Mansa Musa

A Captivating Guide to the Emperor of the Islamic Mali Empire in West Africa and How He Developed Timbuktu into a Major Center for Trade

© Copyright 2021

All Rights Reserved. No part of this book may be reproduced in any form without permission in writing from the author. Reviewers may quote brief passages in reviews.

Disclaimer: No part of this publication may be reproduced or transmitted in any form or by any means, mechanical or electronic, including photocopying or recording, or by any information storage and retrieval system, or transmitted by email without permission in writing from the publisher.

While all attempts have been made to verify the information provided in this publication, neither the author nor the publisher assumes any responsibility for errors, omissions or contrary interpretations of the subject matter herein.

This book is for entertainment purposes only. The views expressed are those of the author alone, and should not be taken as expert instruction or commands. The reader is responsible for his or her own actions.

Adherence to all applicable laws and regulations, including international, federal, state and local laws governing professional licensing, business practices, advertising and all other aspects of doing business in the US, Canada, UK or any other jurisdiction is the sole responsibility of the purchaser or reader.

Neither the author nor the publisher assumes any responsibility or liability whatsoever on the behalf of the purchaser or reader of these materials. Any perceived slight of any individual or organization is purely unintentional.

Free Bonus from Captivating History (Available for a Limited time)

Hi History Lovers!

Now you have a chance to join our exclusive history list so you can get your first history ebook for free as well as discounts and a potential to get more history books for free! Simply visit the link below to join.

Captivatinghistory.com/ebook

Also, make sure to follow us on Facebook, Twitter and Youtube by searching for Captivating History.

Contents

INTRODUCTION: A GOLDEN EMPEROR IN A GOLDEN AGE.................1
CHAPTER 1 - THE FOREFATHERS OF MANSA MUSA......................5
CHAPTER 2 - MANSA MUSA COMES TO THE THRONE....................17
CHAPTER 3 - MANSA MUSA GETS READY FOR THE HAJJ 22
CHAPTER 4 - AND THEY'RE OFF! 29
CHAPTER 5 - MANSA MUSA MAKES HIS MOVE........................34
CHAPTER 6 - IN THE LAND OF EGYPT 41
CHAPTER 7 - MANSA RESUMES HIS PILGRIMAGE......................50
CHAPTER 8 - HEADING BACK HOME 56
CHAPTER 9 - RETURN TO THE CAPITAL...................................62
CHAPTER 10 - MALI AFTER MANSA MUSA 67
CONCLUSION: THE LEGACY OF AN EMPIRE 82
HERE'S ANOTHER BOOK BY CAPTIVATING HISTORY THAT
YOU MIGHT LIKE 86
FREE BONUS FROM CAPTIVATING HISTORY (AVAILABLE FOR
A LIMITED TIME) 87
APPENDIX A: FURTHER READING AND REFERENCE.................88

Introduction: A Golden Emperor in a Golden Age

His proud and regal face stares out at us from old medieval maps, donning a golden crown and holding a golden globe in the palm of his hand. There is just something very special about the West African monarch named Mansa Musa, who lived during the High Middle Ages. The Catalan Atlas, which features the illustrated image of Mansa Musa, was actually drawn up in 1375, several decades after Mansa Musa had already passed. Contrary to its name, the book isn't actually an atlas, as it just contains one map.

The fact that Mansa Musa was still remembered all those years later—remembered enough to put his face on a map—indicates just how stunning a figure Mansa Musa really was. The Catalan Atlas, composed by a Spanish, more specifically Majorcan, cartographer named Abraham Cresques, was a standard and mainstay for medieval explorers. Cresques had been hired by Prince John of Aragon to create a map of the known world.

This was, of course, over one hundred years before the American continents were known (excluding the Vikings' jaunt to Canada), so the "known world" of those days, at least among Europeans, primarily consisted of Europe, Asia, and Africa. It was on the portion of the

Catalan Atlas that designated West Africa that we find the intriguing illustration of Mansa Musa, who is seated on a throne with a nugget of pure gold in his raised hand.

All of the subsequent intrepid explorers who saw the noble visage of Mansa Musa staring back at them as they did their best to use the Catalan Atlas to navigate through unknown lands and waters must have wondered just who this great African king was. Although there is still much that has yet to be uncovered about Mansa Musa's life, fortunately, through the piecing together of historical records, Mali lore, and archaeological finds, that once puzzling picture has become a little clearer.

Mansa Musa ruled from his throne in his capital city of Niani, which literally sat right on top of a gold mine. In those days, Mali is believed to have had some of the largest gold deposits in the world, and Mansa Musa's successful stewardship of these resources—according to modern estimates—most likely made him the richest man who ever lived. Mansa Musa is, in fact, estimated to have had a net worth that would be very near four hundred billion dollars in today's US currency.

Just to put that into perspective, the current richest human being on the planet (at least as of this writing) is a man named Elon Musk. Musk has a net worth of almost 200 billion dollars. It is indeed rather incredible to think that even with all of the resources and commercial expertise of the modern world today, our current richest figure is worth only roughly half of what this little-known Malian emperor—Mansa Musa—had at his disposal in the Middle Ages.

"Disposal" is perhaps the best word to describe Mansa Musa's monetary capacity since he was so rich, he was able to dispose of his riches at a moment's notice and in any way he pleased. Although much of his life is shrouded in mystery, one of the most memorable moments of his existence occurred when he visited Cairo while on the hajj and managed to singlehandedly crash the gold markets! He did this through purchases as well as blatant generosity. Just imagine this

West African ruler arriving in Cairo, Egypt, and handing out gold bars to random people on the street as if it were nothing!

Mansa Musa unloaded so much gold in Egypt that it sunk the value of this precious metal in the Egyptian economy, and the repercussions lasted over a decade after Mansa Musa's departure. After all, gold is valuable because of its scarcity. So, if everyone you know suddenly has a pile of gold in their lap, this rare metal is not worth quite as much anymore.

Mali had more gold than anywhere else in the world at this time, and the sudden unloading of a large quantity of it in Egypt kicked off a spate of hyperinflation that put the Egyptian merchants and financial brokers to shame. It was this exploit more than anything else that sent shockwaves through the Middle East, across the Mediterranean, and on into Europe. Soon, many heads of state around the world were whispering about the mysterious Mali emperor who had so much gold that he did not quite know what to do with it.

But after returning from his hajj, Mansa Musa did make some very wise investments. In 1324, while Musa was still abroad during his hajj, his top general, Sagamandia, had managed to annex two major trading cities—Gao and Timbuktu—to the realm. Mansa Musa used all of the resources at his disposal to make these two West African metropolises stand out as not only centers of immense commerce and trade but also of learning.

He hired top-of-the-line architects to build mosques, schools, and government buildings, some of which still stand to this day. Subsequent explorers, such as the famed Muslim scholar Ibn Battuta, later visited these sites and marveled at their construction. The (Islamic school) of Sankore, which would ultimately become the University of Sankore, would draw thousands of dedicated students and boasted a library that housed countless scholastic texts and valuable manuscripts.

Mansa Musa not only wanted to enrich his empire with material wealth but also with a legacy of learning and education. It was these efforts that would leave the most lasting imprint on his empire. Long after the gold was gone and the salt mines may have dried up, these storied centers of knowledge remain fixed in the sands of the desert regions of Gao and Timbuktu, just as they are fixed in the sands of time.

In all, Mansa Musa ruled the Mali Empire for twenty-five years, and by all accounts, he was entirely beloved by his people. According to Arab historian Ibn Kathir, he was a dashing, charismatic, and charming figure. Ibn Kathir described Mansa Musa as being "a young, handsome man, who had 24 kings under his authority." Under Mansa Musa's rule, these subordinate kings would serve as governors for a sprawling empire that took up much of West Africa. And as the Catalan Atlas can attest, the Mali Empire was West Africa.

Mansa Musa reigned over a vast empire. He wore a golden crown, carried golden weapons, sat on a grand throne, and held firm to a golden staff. It is really no wonder that he was known as the golden emperor. It truly was a golden age for Mali and, by extension, a golden age for the whole world.

Chapter 1 – The Forefathers of Mansa Musa

"I have the mohawk. I don't wanna be disrespectful to the Mohican Indians but there is a tribe in Africa called the Mandinka warriors. They're in the west coast of Africa in the country of Mali. I was reading National Geographic Magazine back in 1977, and I saw the warrior standing there with his spear and his beads around his neck and whatnot, and the stuff on his ankles. That was what gave me the idea, I said, 'Wow, let me bring respect to them,' so basically what I wear is called a Mandinka cut."

-Mr. T

From the very beginning of recorded history, the African continent has always been held as a place of mystery and wonder. The prospect of obtaining wondrous wealth in the form of Africa's sub-Saharan gold deposits has long brought various parties from far and wide. As early as 400 CE, local African kingdoms found themselves in a power struggle over who would control this wealth. And by around 800 CE, it was the Kingdoms of Ghana, Songhai (also sometimes spelled as "Songhay"), and Mali, in particular, that began to rule the region.

Of these kingdoms, Ghana began to dominate early on, with the Kingdom of Mali as a client state. When the Kingdom of Ghana went into decline, Mali became the dominant player in the region. Mali then reached empire status in the 900s, and it would become its most powerful during the 1200s, by which time it had supplanted the Kingdom of Ghana entirely. During Mali's reign as the greatest empire of West Africa, one of the most prominent rulers was a man named Sundiata Keita (also sometimes called Mari Diata, Mari Djata, or Mari Jata).

Most of what we know of Sundiata Keita comes down to us through oral history, which has been passed down from one generation to the next. The purveyors of this oral history belonged to a specialized group of Mali storytellers called the griots. It was the griots who were charged with committing important historical events to memory and also typically served as advisors to their rulers.

According to griot lore, Sundiata was the son of the princess Sogolon Conde and King Nare Maghann Konate. The griot lore records that both Sundiata and his mother, Sogolon Conde, were cruelly mocked and ridiculed by their peers. Sogolon was apparently the object of ridicule because of her appearance. She was actually described as being an "ugly hunchback" with huge eyeballs that bulged out of her head.

The griot lore passed down to us also contends that Sogolon was a powerful sorceress who could shapeshift into animal forms. As the story goes, when she grew weary of being a hunchbacked woman, she would transform into a humpbacked buffalo of all things. Another version of the tale says that Sogolon actually became cursed after she killed her sister in a fit of rage. At any rate, if Sogolon was supposedly so horrible, frightening, and downright atrocious, one might naturally wonder why did King Nare Maghann Konate marry her?

The reason was quite simple. Nare Maghann Konate's own soothsayers foretold that if he married "an ugly woman," she would give birth to a powerful king. In following this lead, Nare Maghann Konate set about searching for the "ugly woman" that his diviners had foretold. He was later convinced that it was none other than Sogolon Conde, as she fit that description.

Having such a reputation was certainly not flattering, to say the least. But Sogolon Conde, despite her rough physical appearance, seemed to have some level of at least cautious respect from the masses. She was, after all, said to be a powerful sorceress. Having said that, most did not really want to get on her bad side lest she cast some sort of spell on them. But if Nare Maghann Konate expected her to birth a child who would jump up out of the cradle as someone clearly destined for future greatness, he would be sorely disappointed.

The pregnancy was apparently a difficult one, and it is said to have lasted an unusually long amount of time. Some griot lore, in fact, speaks of Sogolon for being pregnant for over a year! Whatever the case may be, when Sogolon finally gave birth to Sundiata, it was clear that he would have a challenging existence, as Sundiata was seemingly dealt a difficult hand in life due to a childhood illness that left him "crippled" and unable to walk without assistance.

There was no such thing as political correctness in those days, and according to griot oral testimony, Sundiata was mercilessly teased over his disability. In fact, it seemed that the people came to believe that Sundiata deserved the affliction due to his mother's own dark magic, and they assumed the child was essentially cursed. The idea that those with deformities and disabilities are cursed is, sadly, a long-running theme in many West African cultures. To this very day, you can find villages in Mali where children suffering from birth defects such as a cleft lip are routinely mocked and/or shunned by those who feel it was the hands of fate (or a witch) who cleft their lip rather than mere genetic happenstance. It goes without saying that such harsh treatment would be devastating for any child wishing to grow up and do something productive with their life, let alone someday become a great leader.

And as it pertains to Sundiata, the griots are quite clear that Sundiata's neighbors really did believe that there was something terribly wrong with him. In fact, they not only believed it but also resented him for it. This feeling of resentment was then reinforced after Sogolon gave birth to Sundiata's little sister, Kolonkan, and his little brother, Bori, who both apparently turned out healthy and robust while Sundiata remained severely challenged. To resent a child for birth defects he had no control over seems rather despicable, especially from today's viewpoint, but this is apparently what happened.

Nevertheless, Sundiata used the mockery that he was bombarded with to encourage himself, and one day, out of sheer determination, he suddenly rose to his feet and forced himself to walk. The villagers viewed this happenstance as nothing short of a miraculous sign. From this day forward, rather than being mocked, Sundiata became a well-respected member of the community. For a time, it seemed that the hardship of Sundiata's past was behind him.

But when his father, Nare Maghann Konate, abruptly passed away, the young man's life would take another sharp turn. After the passing of his father, Sundiata's political opponents began to plot and scheme for the throne. Soon, he and his family were once again the targets of malicious abuse. Things got so bad that Sogolon Conde took Sundiata and his siblings and fled the country. Sogolon basically grabbed her kids, had them carry whatever they could on their backs, and ran.

This led to an exodus through many regions of what was then the Ghana Empire. In their quest for safe asylum, they eventually made their way to a place called Mema, whose king finally granted them the safety and security that they sought. The king of Mema is said to have become quite close to Sundiata during his stay, and he came to see great potential in the young prince. Eventually, the king decided to offer Sundiata a job. He made Sundiata a royal official in his realm.

And while Sundiata was working in this capacity for the king of Mema, word was sent that the Mandinka people of Mali had been defeated by the Kingdom of Sosso. Emissaries were sent, hoping that Sundiata, whom some had previously prophesied would be a great leader, would come and rescue them.

Belief is indeed a powerful thing. Sundiata's deceased father had died still believing the promise of his soothsayers that his son, Sundiata, was destined for great things. In the society that Sundiata came from, the proclamations of those perceived to be prophets were considered sacrosanct and beyond dispute. Thus, Sundiata's fellow countrymen began to believe in the fate that had been prophesied for Sundiata as well. It is indeed rather ironic that the man who many rejected and was driven out of his own country would be beseeched in such a manner when the chips were down, but according to griot lore, this is precisely what happened.

Sundiata could have simply ignored those who called for his aid and lived quite happily in the courts of the king of Mema. By this time, his mother, Sogolon, had perished. It is not entirely clear how she died, but it seems to have been of natural causes during their stay at the Mema court. At any rate, her passing potentially could have had the effect of erasing any last connection her adult son may have had to his ancestral homeland. Why should he rush in and help those who had been so cruel to him and his family? Was the pull of his prophesized greatness really enough to make him return to such a hateful place? But Sundiata was not one to hold petty grievances, and ancestral fealty ran deep within him. Feeling the call of destiny, he agreed to liberate those he still considered to be his people.

Sundiata was able to cobble together an army courtesy of the Mema king, and with these troops, he launched his liberation campaign of Mali. These troops then hooked up with the remaining independent warlords of Mali to root out the Sosso conquerors. The Sosso were ultimately destroyed at the Battle of Kirina, an engagement that took place in the Koulikoro Region of Mali, and as a result, Sundiata became the first emperor or mansa of the Mali Empire. The actual battle itself is believed to have taken place sometime around the year 1230 CE.

Although the details are rather scant, the Battle of Kirina was said to have been a cataclysmic event in which two powerful armies relentlessly smashed into each other. It is said that during this conflict, Sundiata managed to kill Sumanguru Kante, the Sosso king himself, with a poison-tipped arrow. Some versions of the story, however, claim that after Sundiata discovered that Sumanguru's spirit animal was a "rooster," he fixed a "cock's spur" to his arrow and fired it at Sumanguru.

Legend tells that the brave Sundiata attached the bird's clawed foot to the end of an arrow, pulled back his bow, and sent the improvised missile hurling toward Sumanguru. The arrow itself did not do much damage. All this clawed arrow did was nick the warlord, but supposedly, it knocked down the magical protective shield that had heretofore kept him from harm.

According to this version of the story, Sumanguru, who was an accomplished sorcerer, was virtually invulnerable in battle until Sundiata managed to discover this one chink in his spiritual armor. After this, it is suggested that Sumanguru was either killed or was otherwise somehow defeated (some versions suggest he was even magically turned to stone).

Yes, griot lore insists that both sides made great use of magic and witchcraft against their enemy. Sundiata was supposedly the son of a sorceress, so it would have only seemed fitting for such dark arts to have been used. Such things are, no doubt, hard for a modern reader to believe, but the mention of wizardry and witchcraft serves as a good demonstration of what the belief systems were in those days. This was, of course, before Islam became the religion of the land or at least of the ruling classes. Prior to Islam, most people in the region practiced ancestral shamanism.

At any rate, once the battle had been won, and both Sumanguru's castle and his "magic tower" were burned down, the victorious Sundiata made his capital at Niani, a strategic location fixed between modern-day Mali's border with Guinea. His empire would come to dominate almost all of West Africa. Sundiata's armies easily conquered the territory of what had been the old Ghana Empire, as well as added additional territory in what is today modern Senegal, Gambia, and Guinea Bissau.

The Mali Empire would come to control all of the important trade routes, which stretched from the rain forests to the south all the way to the Saharan deserts of North Africa. This allowed the leaders of Mali to control the gold trade as it was taken from the south to the north. Camels laden with gold traveling back and forth through the Mali Empire to places far and wide would soon become a common occurrence.

The interesting thing about how Mansa Sundiata handled his empire is that he chose to run the large tracts of the territory he gained as a federation. Rather than having top-heavy centralized control, he allowed each region to have its own local administrator who would handle local affairs, even though each administrator reported to the emperor (or the mansa) as the ultimate authority.

The Mali Empire also established what was known as the "Great Gbara Assembly," which was a form of parliament that placed a check on the emperor lest he overstep his bounds. It was rather forward-thinking of the Mali Empire to have such a system of checks and balances in place. Most kings and queens of the Middle Ages ruled through "might makes right," whereas the Mali mansas had to make sure that their actions lined up with the Great Gbara Assembly.

The mansa was powerful for sure, but thanks to the Great Gbara Assembly, they were still held accountable for their actions all the same. The Great Gbara Assembly even had the power to remove the emperor if need be, and it was up to the assembly to designate the successor of the previous mansa. As it pertains to the man who became Mansa Sundiata, he successfully reigned within the bounds of this system for some twenty-five years.

Although it is not entirely clear what ultimately befell Sundiata, griot lore seems to indicate that he was the victim of a tragic accident. One version of events insists that he fell into a river, but another speaks of him accidentally being hit by an arrow—a poison arrow, in fact. Could it have been the wicked sorcerer king Sumanguru whom Sundiata had previously struck down, exacting his final revenge from beyond the grave? It certainly makes for a good story to tell around the campfire. But no one, not even those wise Mali heralds, the griots, seems to really know for sure.

But whatever may have happened, after his passing, Mansa Sundiata was ultimately succeeded by his son Uli (sometimes spelled as Ali or Wali). Mansa Uli was known as a powerful, successful ruler who expanded his reach all the way to the important commercial hub of Timbuktu. It is important to note that he did not annex Timbuktu outright (this would happen later), but he did make Timbuktu a part of the general Mali orbit.

He is also notable for converting to Islam and being the first mansa to undergo the hajj, a religious pilgrimage to Mecca, the holy city of Islam. It is recorded that he made his pilgrimage to Saudi Arabia during the time when a certain sultan named Baybars (or Baibars) reigned in Egypt, and Uli made his presence known when passing through Baybars's land. Mansa Uli's reign would last until the year 1270.

The next person to be selected as the mansa of Mali was Uli's brother, Wati. Mansa Wati would prove to be far less successful than his predecessors and would only remain in power for four years. It was after Mansa Wati's short rule that control of the Mali Empire fell upon the shoulders of another of Sundiata's descendants, this time, an adopted son named Khalifa. But Khalifa, who had a penchant for randomly shooting people with arrows (this was apparently a hobby of his), was quickly proven unfit to rule.

Cruel, insane, and tyrannical are the best adjectives to describe Khalifa, and it wasn't long before Khalifa was removed from power. The next man chosen for the job of mansa by the Great Gbara Assembly was Sundiata's grandson Abu Bakr (or Abubakari). It seems that Abu Bakr I was more or less a stooge for the elites, and he is thought to have been a kind of "puppet ruler" put in place by the assembly. Abu Bakr I would run the empire for twelve years before he was replaced in 1285 by a man named Sakura.

Of all the mansas so far, Sakura has one of the most unique stories, as he was apparently a former slave. Some sources also state that he was a military commander of some sort. Such transitions are not uncommon in African civilizations, and even former slaves often found opportunities to rise through the ranks. In fact, one of the most famous African slaves to rise to prominence is documented in none other than the Bible, although it must be noted that not all of the tales of the Old Testament have been historically validated. Regardless, if one considers the Bible, Prophet Joseph, who was enslaved in Egypt, later become one of the pharaoh's top commanders.

At any rate, Sakura—the former slave turned military leader—staged a successful coup that removed Abu Bakr I from power. Even though his seizure of power was illegal, he proved to be such a good leader that the political powers that be allowed him to remain mansa. He was indeed a steady hand at the helm, and under his leadership, the borders of the Mali Empire began to stretch eastward to the region of Gao, a region that would later be officially annexed under Mansa Musa.

Outside forces, however, would intervene, and Sakura's rein would come to an end in 1300 when he was murdered while returning home from Mecca. Traveling across the Sahara Desert was certainly not easy to begin with, and it wasn't uncommon for Bedouin bandits to make it even harder. Sakura's body was recovered, however, and it is recorded that Sakura was buried with full honor, befitting of a great Mali emperor. After Sakura, the next leader put forth by the assembly as mansa was a man named Gao, who was one of Kolonkan's sons. Kolonkan, if you don't remember, was Sundiata Keita's younger sister.

Mansa Gao's reign was another brief one, of which very little is recorded. After his reign came to an end, the power then passed to his son, Mohammad ibn Goa, in 1305 (although some sources state the year as being 1307). Mansa Mohammad was succeeded by a nephew of Sundiata, Abu Bakr (or Abubakri) II. Abu Bakr II is an intriguing individual because, according to legend, he actually sent a large expedition—large as in some two hundred ships—across the Atlantic in order to see what was on the other side.

This voyage allegedly occurred nearly two centuries before Christopher Columbus tried the same feat. According to tradition, of these two hundred ships that were sent out, only one returned. But the stories that this one returned vessel conveyed were so wonderous that Abu Bakr immediately prepared for a follow-up mission in which he himself would take part. This time, he went all out and prepared a fleet of two thousand ships, an armada that he would personally lead. Just before he left, however, he made sure Musa (also sometimes known as Kankan Musa) was named as his successor.

As the story goes, Abu Bakr II never found his way back. As the Mali ruler was thought to be lost for all time, Musa became the new leader (or mansa) of the empire, thus becoming Mansa Musa. The story of how Mansa Musa came to the throne is perhaps hard to believe. But as fanciful as it all might sound, it was a narrative that Mansa Musa himself repeated. An Arab scholar by the name of Al Umari actually recorded the words of Mansa Musa as he recalled this very sequence of events.

Mansa Musa allegedly explained:

The ruler who preceded me did not believe that it was impossible to reach the extremity of the ocean that encircles the earth, and wanted to reach that [the extremity] and obstinately persisted in the design. So he equipped two hundred boats full of men, like many others full of gold, water and victuals [food] sufficient enough for several years. He ordered the chief not to return until they had reached the extremity of the ocean, or if they had exhausted the provisions and the water. They set out. Their absence extended over a long period, and, at last, only one boat returned. On our questioning, the captain said: "Prince, we have navigated for a long time, until we saw in the midst of the ocean as if a big river was flowing violently. My boat was the last one; others were ahead of me. As soon as any of them reached this place, it drowned in the whirlpool and never came out. I sailed backwards to escape this current." But the Sultan would not believe him. He ordered two thousand boats to be equipped for him and for his men, and one thousand more for water and victuals. Then he conferred on me the regency during his absence, and departed with his men on the ocean trip, never to return nor to give a sign of life.

If this legend is true, one must wonder what actually happened to these Mali voyagers. Were they sucked up in a whirlpool? Prior to Columbus finding the New World and proving the nature of our round globe, many ordinary people actually believed that sailing across the Atlantic too far would cause one to fall right off the edge of the planet!

Whatever may have happened to Abu Bakr and his men, they were certainly brave enough to chart a course for the unknown. And the story doesn't end there because there are some who claim that these Mali explorers—at least those who didn't get sucked up in a whirlpool—actually made it all the way to at least one of the American continents.

Although its currently nothing more than pure conjecture, fueled by various anecdotal threads, some historians, such as Ivan Van Sertima, who was an expert on African history, have theorized that it might have been possible that these wayward explorers from Mali set up a colony in what's now known as modern-day Brazil.

One odd anomaly that seems to give credence to the notion of pre-Columbian contact with and travel to the Americas is the fact that archaeologists have long been baffled by discoveries of purely American produce being found in Old World archaeological sites where they shouldn't be. Just take the so-called "nicotine" mummies as a good example of this strange occurrence. In Egypt, mummies have been discovered that have remnants of nicotine on their person. As funny as the idea of smoking mummies might sound, the crazy thing is tobacco originated from the Americas. And according to the official narrative, no one in the Old World had tobacco until after Christopher Columbus. Yet, the nicotine mummies and other archaeological sites seem to defy this logic with their deposits of American goods that date back to pre-Columbian times.

However, critics are sure to assert that the nicotine may have found its way to the mummies through other more prosaic means, such as by way of an archaeologist or two who smoked heavily at a dig site and thereby contaminated the mummies. At any rate, whatever the case may be, it was due to the failure of Abu Bakr II to return from his epic trip across the Atlantic that Mansa Musa came to the imperial throne.

Chapter 2 – Mansa Musa Comes to the Throne

"And has the story of Musa come to you? When he saw fire, he said to his family: Stop, for surely I see a fire, haply I may bring to you therefrom a live coal or find a guidance at the fire. So when he came to it, a voice was uttered: Oh Musa! Surely I am your Lord, therefore put off our shoes; surely you are in the sacred valley, Tuwa. And I have chosen you, so listen to what is revealed. Surely I am Allah, there is no god but I, therefore serve me and keep up prayer for remembrance. Surely the hour is coming—I am about to make it manifest—so that every soul may be rewarded as it strives."

-Surah Taha 20: 9-15 (The Quran)

It is said that the Mali Empire, at its greatest extent, stretched from the Atlantic Ocean all the way to Lake Chad. This is a big chunk of western and part of central Africa. With it came great resources but also great responsibility. Mansa Musa's imperial leadership of the Mali Empire is said to have begun around the year 1312. For it was in this year that Mansa Musa was installed inside the imperial palace at the Mali capital of Niani, where he ruled alongside his queen and wife, Inari Kunate.

In the Mali Empire, it was common for the mansa to have a main wife, such as Inari Kunate, who would be considered the queen, along with additional wives who did not share that distinction. Not too much is known about Mansa Musa's royal bride Inari Kunate other than the fact that she eventually bore him a son by the name of Maghan. Mansa Maghan's later rule after his father's death is equally obscure, especially since it is basically just a footnote compared to his father's legacy. Some sources say that Mansa Maghan ruled for just a few years before he died.

At any rate, as it pertains to Mansa Musa, it was from his palace in Niani—the capital city of Mali—that the great mansa oversaw all the happenings of his realm. Here, he could be seen seated on a "grand seat of ebony, flanked by elephant tusks" as his court ministers kept him abreast of all of the latest developments. When the emperor sat on his grand throne, he was always flanked by his imperial retinue.

The interesting thing about the way the court system of the Mali Empire worked was the fact that it made use of an official "spokesman" who spoke on behalf of the emperor. The emperor himself was never directly spoken to. Any inquiries were always given to his intermediary, who then personally presented them to the mansa. The mansa then gave his response to the intermediary spokesman, who repeated it back to those who had inquired in the first place.

It's admittedly not the most efficient means of communicating with a sovereign, but it served the purpose of keeping the mansa's position as one that was especially revered and distinct. Another sign that those in an audience with the emperor were dealing with someone of authority was the fact that no one was allowed to wear sandals in his presence. This meant that those gathered around the mansa had to be barefoot at all times. Being in the presence of the mansa was considered so sacred, in fact, that even sneezing was barred! Yes, it was actually forbidden to sneeze in the presence of the mansa of Mali, and if the ruler himself happened to get a case of the sniffles, it was customary for all who were present to beat their chest as if they themselves were the ones with the cold. By displaying complete solidarity with their sovereign, the people showed that if their leader suffered, they suffered as well.

Mansa Musa was also always surrounded by a bodyguard unit, which was composed of his own personal slaves. Yes, Mansa Musa had slaves, but it is important to note that slavery in his realm and in many other parts of Africa was much different than how it came to be practiced in other parts of the world. In Mali, slaves, although subject to their owners, were not usually cruelly treated or discriminated against, and they were often given important tasks to fulfill at court, such as being the mansa's personal spokesman or as a griot, the historians of the court.

To be clear, the concept of owning another human being is wrong in all of its forms. But the nature of slavery in Mali was also clearly different than how it would later manifest in the trans-Atlantic slave trade or even the Arab slave trade. Both Europeans and Arabs tended to dehumanize their slaves, whereas indigenous slavery in West Africa was viewed as more of a temporary social class distinction. Having said that, slaves had a much greater chance of rising above their lowly station, as can be seen in the case of one of Mali's most renowned emperors, Mansa Sakura. Despite his former status of being a slave, Mansa Sakura rose to the top rung of Malian society. As long as he performed as an able and competent leader, which he apparently did, no one had any qualms with his previous condition.

It is said that the Mali Empire, in fact, had an official "prohibition" on any mistreatment of both enemy combatants or slaves for any reason. This does not mean that slaves were never mistreated; on some occasions, they most likely were. There are always mean and cruel people in the world who desire to treat others badly if they are given the opportunity. But the official stance of the kingdom was to treat slaves in what was deemed to be a fair manner.

One of the first edicts of import issued by Mansa Musa occurred during his first year on the throne when he decreed that Islam would be the Mali Empire's state religion. Prior to the determination to make Mali a Muslim empire, most of the people believed in African ancestral beliefs, but with Mansa Musa's order, Islam would become the religious standard of the land.

This doesn't mean that people abandoned their prior religious beliefs overnight. In fact, many kept practicing their native traditions even after this ordinance went out. Mansa Musa himself made it clear that although Islam was considered the official state religion, he would more or less tolerate other beliefs in his kingdom. And he certainly wasn't going to force anyone to unwillingly become a Muslim if they did not wish to do so. Had he tried, it no doubt would have sparked a rebellion among the lower classes, as they especially clung to their ancestral religion.

Mansa Musa was a shrewd enough ruler to know that nothing good would have come from such forced conversion. In allowing his subjects to retain their beliefs, he also showed a bit of latent superstition of his own. For Mansa Musa, through his observations, had come to the conclusion that the gold mines controlled by those who still practiced ancestral beliefs produced more gold than those who had converted to Islam.

Certainly, there must have been a rational explanation for this. Mansa Musa himself hit upon it in a later offhand remark that was recorded for posterity when he said something to the effect of "free people are more productive than those under duress." But whatever the case may be, Mansa Musa also took it as a sign that the gold mines under pagan administration were best left with their traditional mode of religion lest he somehow jinx the cash flow of the kingdom.

Many of the locals actually believed that a snake god was the force behind the gold deposits, and they routinely made the worship of this deity a centerpiece to their mining operations. Some sources even suggest that human sacrifice might have been carried out in the past in order to please the spirits. It is said that the gold miners in Mali were convinced that digging up gold was literally a matter of life and death in which both the living and the deceased took part.

But despite many in the lower classes sticking to more traditional beliefs, the upper classes embraced Islam as being the proper religious standard-bearer of the realm. Islam was seen as a vehicle to the upper crust of society. Converting the empire to Islam was also important for relations with Mali's neighbors in northern Africa, especially Morocco, since they too had long ago found their way into the house of Islam. Mali was now a member of the Muslim world, and its trade of commerce and culture would only benefit as a result.

Arab traders were, of course, a major part of the trading network in Africa, and since Mali's conversion, they felt more or less right at home in the Muslim Mali Empire. After making Islam the official religion of the empire, Mansa Musa furthered the Islamization of his realm by building several mosques, many with impressive minarets that reached the sky. From these houses of worship, the faithful would hear the call for prayer. Bearing testament to their solid architecture, some of these mosques are still in use to this very day.

But as great as his personal faith was while at home, since Mansa Musa was a Muslim, he was required to make the traditional hajj, or pilgrimage, to the holy city of Mecca in modern-day Saudi Arabia. Making a pilgrimage to Mecca is one of the Five Pillars of Islam, which all Muslims are meant to fulfill. The other pillars, simply put, are faith, prayer, worship, fasting, and alms-giving. So, if one is a dedicated Muslim, there is just no way of getting around the obligation of the hajj. No matter how far they may be from this centerpiece of Islam, all of the Muslim faithful are expected to reach Mecca at some point in their lifetime, that is, as long as they are able to make the arduous journey. And Mansa Musa's own personal journey would create an epic odyssey like no other.

Chapter 3 – Mansa Musa Gets Ready for the Hajj

"During the past eleven days here in the Muslim world, I have eaten from the same plate, drunk from the same glass and slept on the same rug—while praying to the same God—with fellow Muslims whose eyes were the bluest of the blue, whose hair was the blondest of blond, and whose skin was the whitest of white. And in the words and in the deeds of the white Muslims, I felt the same sincerity that I felt among the black African Muslims of Nigeria, Sudan and Ghana."

-Malcolm X

The hajj is a trip that all faithful Muslims are required to make at least once in their lifetime if they are able to. No matter where they live, those who have dedicated themselves to the hajj must make their way to the holy city of Mecca in Saudi Arabia. Since the Muslim faithful gather in this one spot from all corners of the Earth, the term "mecca" has become synonymous with the concept of an ultimate "gathering place" of enthusiasts. Just imagine being at a comic or science fiction convention, for example, and the comic-book-reading fan next to you suddenly exclaims, "By Jove! This is a real mecca for comic book fans!" Well, my friends, it is the very nature of the hajj, which drew people to this one city, that has caused the name of Mecca itself to become a descriptive term for a gathering place.

Those who successfully complete this journey are given the honorary title of being a hajji. For Mansa Musa, his journey would be an epic one that would take him through the deserts of North Africa, into Egypt, and then on into Saudi Arabia. He would cover over nine thousand miles, and the journey itself would take over a year to complete. There are a few alternating tales as to what inspired Mansa Musa to journey to Mecca when he did. One of the more intriguing narratives actually makes the claim that Mansa Musa "accidentally" killed his own mother, Nana Gongo (sometimes also called Kankou or Kanku).

According to this version of Mansa Musa lore, her death was apparently the result of some kind of freak accident, and Mansa Musa was horrified at what had happened. As intriguing as this happenstance seems to be, the traditional sources are strangely quiet as to just what kind of "accident" may have befallen Mansa Musa's mother. If this event really did occur, it would seem that Musa's family was somehow plagued with all kinds of bad luck. His ancestor Sundiata, after all, is also believed to have perished from an accidental death.

At any rate, in his grief, Musa tried to make amends by giving an excessive amount of alms to the poor. But when he still felt guilty about the whole ordeal, he turned to an Islamic cleric for advice. The cleric advised Mansa Musa that he should head off to Mecca and "seek sanctuary with the Prophet" so that he could request him to "intervene on his behalf with Allah."

Some other versions of the story indicate that his soothsayers simply gave him a random day on the calendar with which to begin his journey. According to West African historian David C. Conrad, the diviners, without much rhyme or reason, "told Mansa Musa he should wait until a Saturday that would fall on the 12th day of the month. This meant that he had to wait nine months before he could leave—which he did."

At any rate, he became motivated to go. In order to prepare for the trip, Mansa Musa went all out as far as provisions were concerned. He collected goods from all over the Mali Empire, and he also gathered up the best teachers and scholars that he could find to accompany him on the journey. In the end, Mansa Musa's retinue would consist of some sixty thousand subjects, with twelve thousand of them said to be members of Mansa's imperial court. He also took his wife, royal Queen Inari Kunate, with him, although their son, Maghan, stayed behind to function as the acting mansa in his father's absence.

Others who undertook the perilous journey of the hajj often had to risk their own lives traveling treacherous roads on which bandits preyed upon travelers. But Mansa Musa, with a veritable army surrounding him (eight thousand men in the group were soldiers), did not have to worry so much about banditry. All the bandits could do was watch with envy as Mansa Musa's camels carted some twenty-four thousand pounds of gold. Yes, Mansa Musa practically took a whole storehouse of gold with him.

In fact, Mansa Musa had so much gold that even his servants who accompanied the grand entourage of Mansa Musa's caravan are said to have each had a staff of solid gold in their possession. It must have broken a Bedouin's heart to see such great treasures passing through the desert and being completely unable to plunder it! Considering the great wealth of both gold and advisors that Mansa Musa brought with him, many have since speculated that Mansa Musa was seeking to turn his trip into a diplomatic one, although he was, of course, still going for spiritual reasons as well.

It only makes sense if you think about it. Since Mansa Musa was required by Islamic law to make the hajj to Mecca, he might as well develop strong diplomatic ties along the way. Places like Morocco, Libya, Egypt, and Saudi Arabia would have been important regional players that one should establish political ties with.

It was a big mission, but Mansa Musa didn't forget his responsibilities at home while he was away. As mentioned above, he left his son Maghan in charge, and if he were to fail to return, which had happened when Musa's predecessor, Abu Bakr II, failed to return all those years ago, his son would automatically take over the empire.

With all of these important matters of state squared away, it is said that Mansa Musa left around October, right at the end of the harvest season in the Mali Empire. The day of the mansa's departure was marked as one of celebration, in which all of the citizens took part. According to official lore, people gathered from all corners of the Mali Empire to see the emperor off. There were great speeches made in the emperor's honor, songs were sung, dances were danced, and sacrificial animals were placed upon the altar—all in preparation for the emperor's departure from the land.

Priests and holy men were also much sought after to bless the path of Mansa Musa's journey. It is important to note that although Mansa Musa himself was a Muslim, he, at least at this point in time, heartily embraced all of the various religious strains of his empire. And it is said that all modes of religious sentiment were on display on the day of his departure and that all were utilized in an effort to bless his trip. Considering the fact that some of his predecessors, such as the ill-fated slave-turned-king Mansa Sakura, did not return when they undertook their hajj, Mansa Musa no doubt probably figured he could use all of the blessings he could get.

The oral historians of the Mali Empire, the griots, recorded a rather strange event that allegedly occurred right before the emperor departed from the capital city of Niani. According to them, Mansa Musa requested four birds. Just four regular birds that you typically see singing and chattering away in the overhanging trees. Once these birds were acquired, the mansa then instructed his attendants to kill the birds and cut them up into pieces. Mansa Musa had the chopped-up bird bits scattered over the four hills of Niani. Most today would not enjoy the sight of dismembered birds, but Mansa Musa apparently took his inspiration from the Quran, which speaks of the ancient patriarch Abraham doing much the same thing, placing the dead remains of four birds on four hills.

As Surah 2:260 (The Cow) vividly describes, "And when Ibrahim [Abraham] said: My Lord! Show me how thou givest life to the dead, He [Allah] said: What! And do you not believe? He [Abraham] said: Yes, but that my heart may be at ease. He [Allah] said: Then take four of the birds, then train them to follow you, then place on every mountain a part of them, then call them, they will come to you flying; and know that Allah is Mighty, Wise."

According to the Quran, God (or Allah) then resurrected the birds and had them come flying back to Abraham as a sign. Mansa Musa repeated this practice himself before leaving Niani, and according to legend, he called the birds back to him just as Abraham had done. To the surprise of those assembled, the birds returned to him but not in physical form. Instead, those gathered were shocked to see what looked like birds of pure light flying toward the emperor. They then witnessed "a halo of light too strong for the naked eye" surround their king.

Such things might be a bit too difficult for a modern reader to believe, but the griots attest that it actually happened. And what happens next is even stranger, especially as the griots recorded it from Mansa Musa's own testimony. The emperor claimed that right after the halo of light surrounded him, everything suddenly came to a stop. Mansa Musa allegedly witnessed all of his subjects—every single one of the thousands gathered around him that day—suddenly freeze in place. Even the animals stood completely stock still and motionless.

It was as if someone had suddenly hit the pause button, with everyone standing like lifeless statues. According to Musa, it was as if time had come to a grinding halt for everyone but him. It is said that during this strange supernatural interval, Mansa Musa immediately came to the conclusion that this work was the product of divine intervention, and the great king fell to the ground to humble himself, absolutely certain that he was in the presence of God. Mansa Musa claimed that he was then visited by an angel who spoke to him briefly before he "commanded the birds to return."

The birds that had been chopped to bits miraculously reformed themselves, then joined the halo of light and took off over the horizon. According to Mansa Musa, it was after this feat that the angel vanished, and as if someone had suddenly pressed the play button, life and motion returned to all those around him. To his shock, his subjects and the animals came back to life as if nothing had happened—all of them completely unaware of the missing time they experienced in which they were in a state of suspended animation.

Mansa Musa stared in wonder, lost in the thought that all of those around him had been frozen in time but were completely unaware that it had happened in the first place. Mansa Musa thought to himself, "Where did the souls go during this common sleep?" If this event happened—and admittedly, that's a big if—Mansa Musa was apparently the only one who even knew it had occurred.

If such a thing was alleged by anyone other than the emperor, no one would have believed them. But since the words of their sovereign were considered sacrosanct, when he informed them of this bizarre occurrence, his subjects took it quite seriously. Although the griots were apparently unable to witness it in real time since they too were frozen in place during the event, they took down the words of their king and recorded his account in their oral testimony.

Mansa Musa's journey to Mecca would be full of all kinds of surprises and unexpected events. In Muslim tradition, the journey to Mecca is very much just as important as the arrival. It's a period of reflection and discovery in which the traveler can become more in tune with themselves and their relationship with the divine. Even for a great ruler like Mansa Musa, who had a large company of subjects accompany him, the journey was still an intensely personal one. And, according to the story of Mansa Musa's vision of the revived birds, which had the thousands of people around him suddenly freeze in suspended animation, God supposedly found a way to speak to Musa on a personal level, distinctly tailored just for him and his experience. Then again, if you choose not to believe in the possibility of the supernatural, such visionary experiences could be chalked up to being a combination of dreams or outright hallucination brought on by the heat. Although Mansa Musa and his followers had yet to traverse the vast desert, which is known to bring about mirages, standing out in the heat with no protection would have been enough to perhaps make one a little more prone to hallucinations. Heat stroke, after all, is a very real phenomenon, and its debilitating effects are widely known. But, of course, seeing a sandy mirage that looks like water rather than a sand dune is one thing; seeing thousands of your followers suddenly look like they are doing the mannequin challenge (an internet trend in which folks suddenly freeze in their tracks like mannequins) is another!

At any rate, after all of these festivities and supposed supernatural occurrences came to their conclusion, it is said that Mansa Musa "mounted his black stallion" before signaling to his retinue that he was ready to depart. Then, at his orders, the caravan's "red and yellow flags unfurled," his entourage began to move, and his long journey to Mecca began.

Chapter 4 – And They're Off!

"Their women are of surpassing beauty, and are shown more respect than the men. These people are Muslims, punctilious in observing the hours of prayer, studying the books of law, and memorizing the Koran. Yet their women show no bashfulness before men and do not veil themselves, though they are assiduous in attending prayers. Any man who wishes to marry one of them may do so, but they do not travel with their husbands, and, even if one desire to do so, her family would not allow her to go."

-Ibn Battuta

The emperor's entourage left the seat of the Mali Empire—the city of Niani—and headed east to the city of Mema. This was the same fabled city that Mansa Musa's ancestor, Mansa Sundiata, had sought refuge in when he was exiled from his kingdom. It was the great king of Mema who took the exiled prince in and saw to his needs, allowing Sundiata to gather his strength so that he could one day return in glorious triumph and found what would become the Mali Empire.

Mansa Musa knew this story all too well, thanks to the loyal griots who repeated the legend on a routine basis. Having said that, Mansa Musa most have stood in wonder as he gazed out at Mema's cityscape and pondered how far his empire had come. His forebearers were driven out of the land, but now, he, their descendant, was the master of a mighty domain that stretched from the Atlantic coast in the west all the way to Lake Chad in the central African Sahel.

At any rate, the emperor was a man on a mission, and he could not stay long. After a brief stop in Mema, the emperor led his entourage to the city of Walata (or Oualata), which borders the southernmost extremity of the Sahara Desert. This was a place of intense heat and dryness. There was a sense of barren desolation in this land, interspersed every so often with the rare sight of one or two palm trees. Mansa Musa and his followers would trek some five hundred miles through this desert as they continued to journey on toward their ultimate goal of Mecca.

Even though the emperor was moving away from the center of his empire, he had trustworthy couriers who continually traveled back and forth between him and his capital. It was the messengers' job to deliver important updates and also send official responses back from the emperor. The emperor and his caravan were, for all intents and purposes, a mobile government in itself. In fact, the emperor would assemble his own council on a daily basis in which status reports were given and directives were issued to all those present.

The life of this mobile kingdom went on, and as with any large gathering of people such as this, issues would arise. The mansa's subjects who were with him could get sick or even die while en route, and they would need to be attended to. Funerals most certainly occurred while on the road, and it was required that the mansa's people were given a proper burial, as it was demanded by tradition.

During their journey, the emperor's subjects were by no means idle, and they contributed to various needed tasks, such as fixing worn-out gear, fashioning new clothing, or going to a local market to replenish the reserves of grain and rice. As one can see, everyone had something to do during this long journey. The mansa's encampment also found time to make merry and have fun. It was a common occurrence at the end of a workweek for the emperor to host festivities right there in the desert, during which his best musicians played instruments such as "ten-stringed harps" and beat their drums as singers sang, dancers danced, and griots told stories of the bygone past.

If any random wayfarer in the Sahara saw this spectacle—if they could even believe it wasn't a mirage that they saw emerge in the middle of the desert—they must have been truly amazed at what they bore witness to. But none of these festivities could quite compare to the absolute bonanza that took place to commemorate the emperor's birth. Yes, life went on like it always did while the mansa and his entourage journeyed to Mecca, and when his birthday came to pass during his time in the desert, it was most certainly commemorated like it always would have been.

The emperor's birthday arrived just as his mobile kingdom reached the borders of Gourara. Mansa Musa and his inner court met with Gourara's governor and other important officials. In celebration of the event, fifty head of cattle were slaughtered, and plenty of rice was dished up. Interestingly, the horns of the cattle that were a part of the feast are said to have been dried out and given special preservation techniques, after which the hollowed-out horns had precious stones, herbal ingredients, and even pieces of Quran scripture stuffed inside of them. These were used as charms and as talismans to ward off evil. This was indeed a mixture of ancestral religion with aspects of Islam attached to it. The Quran itself, in fact, would object against such use since Muslim teaching bans the use of idols or talismans of any kind. But like many people around the world who end up mixing a mainstream religion with older folk religions, such hybridization of ideology tends to occur.

For a good example of this in practice today, all one has to do is look to the island of Haiti, where residents incorporate aspects of the West African indigenous religion of Voodou (a separate but related religion to Voodoo) with Catholicism. In Port-au-Prince, Haiti, it is a common sight to see a Voodou priestess create a Voodou shrine with a statue of the biblical Mother Mary sitting right on top. In much the same way, Malians mixed elements of their ancient ancestral religious practices with Islam.

At any rate, with the festivities in place and the good luck charms at the ready, Mansa Musa's birthday celebration was about to begin. To mark the occasion, the so-called "royal orchestra" came together to perform songs that were meant to capture the experience of making a trip across the desert to reach the holy site of Mecca. This was literally traveling music, which made use of the dynamic pounding of drums to represent their footsteps and rhythmic blowing of horns. The music flowed as freely as the wind at their backs.

Along with the musicians, the wild animals roaming about the outskirts of Gourara no doubt added to the mystique as they howled and called out as the evening progressed. The music, of course, was also accompanied by gleeful dancing, which followed the reverberating sounds in a specifically orchestrated manner. It was in the midst of all of this that the great monarch, Mansa Musa, was given his birthday gifts.

Among the gifts bestowed were the customary sacrificial goat, golden jewelry, precious stones, and a specially made talisman that was uniquely crafted for the occasion. It was similar to the other ceremonial animal horns that were prepared that day, but this horn is said to have been encased in silver and filled with dirt delivered from the capital. It, too, also had specially picked scripture from the Quran, which was chosen for the purpose of blessing the journey.

Mansa Musa was then gifted with a brand-new Quran. He was also gifted with plenty of slaves, which was the custom at the time. But as was previously mentioned, while West Africa has had a long history of slavery, it must be pointed out that the conditions and status of slaves were much different among West Africans than it was when Arabs and Europeans later imposed slavery upon West Africans. For one thing, in many indigenous African societies, it wasn't uncommon for slaves to be elevated to fairly high positions. Yes, they were still owned by someone, but they were also allowed some mobility up the social ladder. This was usually not the case when slavery was carried out in many other parts of the world. Much of the time, even if a slave had been freed, their freedoms were severely restricted and curtailed.

As it pertained to Mali, it would take the Malians quite a long time to shake themselves free from their own legacy of enforced servitude. As late as the 1960s, when modern-day Mali first came into being under Malian President Modibo Keita (an actual descendant of Sundiata Keita himself), Mali was still very much struggling to put a stop to the ancestral practice of Malians having bond servants. President Keita launched massive public campaigns, calling upon anyone still considered to be a slave to be freed. But even with government-backed calls for emancipation, the practice has continued in various forms in Mali to this very day. Apparently, such entrenched traditions are hard to remove outright. And sadly enough, slavery may have been moved underground and thus remains off the periphery, but at least in West Africa, it does indeed still exist.

At any rate, once all of these supposed gifts were bestowed upon Mansa Musa at his birthday celebration, the lore tells us that a lone female singer sang the mansa a song to praise all of the good things that he had done and the good things that he was expected to do in the near future. In some ways, it could be said that this theatrical songstress was actually presenting to everyone the Mali version of a "state of the union address" since it was basically a telling—or presentation—of the current state of the empire set to song.

Just think about it. Much like a president would get up before Congress and laud all of their accomplishments for that particular year, along with what they planned to achieve in the next, Mansa Musa's personal bard likewise sang of Musa's achievements, as well as the goals yet to be fulfilled. It was after all of this that those in attendance were finally allowed to take part in the big feast that had been prepared, and they drank and ate in honor of their beloved ruler.

Chapter 5 – Mansa Musa Makes His Move

"They load their camels at late dawn, and march until the sun has risen, its light has become bright in the air, and the heat on the ground has become severe. Then they put their loads down, hobble their camels, unfasten their baggage and stretch awnings to give some shade from the scorching heat and the hot winds of midday. When the sun begins to decline and sink in the west, they set off. They march for the rest of the day, and keep going until nightfall, when they encamp at whatever place they have reached. Thus the traveling of merchants who enter the county of the Sudan is according to this pattern. They do not deviate from it, because the sun kills with its heat those who run the risk of marching at midday."

-Ibn Battuta

After leaving the festivities of Gourara behind, Mansa Musa and his entourage headed back onto the trail. They still had thousands of miles to go, and in between, they stopped at several regions and towns similar to Gourara along the way. Although the mansa's birthday had passed, they were still greeted by frequent celebrations and gift-giving. They were soon halfway to the first major milestone—the oasis of Touat (also spelled as Tuat). The oasis of Touat is located in a North

African region that today lies in the modern-day nation state of Algeria.

In between these two mile markers, Mansa Musa and his traveling party ventured across a landscape that ranged from sand dunes to rough grasslands where wild animals grazed. The emptiness of the countryside was only occasionally interrupted by some ragtag caravan camps or even the occasional stray Bedouin traveler. And as was the case when Mansa Musa and company arrived at the settlement of Teghaza (or Taghaza), they also encountered whole mosques of salt.

This region, in fact, is full of salt mines, and it was not uncommon to find whole houses made out of salt, with perhaps an animal skin roof thrown on top for cover. Once Mansa Musa reached the edge of the oasis of Touat, he and his party celebrated, as the company could finally refill their goatskin bags with fresh water and, for once, could actually rest under the shade of a palm tree or two.

In this region, Mansa Musa also took time to get to know the local leaders. It is said that during these exchanges, Mansa Musa was generous as usual, handing out large amounts of gold coinage to all who sought his audience. In the name of hospitality, he too was given gifts. At one point, he received a precious box filled with pearls. At the oasis, he was given a large supply of a valuable herb called tacarghaut, which is quite renowned for its aroma.

Mansa Musa was also given a tour by the local governor of the wells from which the water of the oasis had sprung. Just before leaving Touat, Mansa Musa took the time to meet with traders who had just arrived from the cities of Fez and Marrakech, located in modern-day Morocco and located just north of where Mansa Musa was at the time. Mansa Musa was interested in both their trade goods and the tales of their travels.

Morocco was an important regional player, and it actually bordered the reaches of Mansa Musa's own kingdom, so he was very much interested in strengthening political and commercial ties with it. Indeed, much of Mansa Musa's life and the lives of several of his successors would be spent prioritizing the diplomatic relations with the Moroccan sultanate above all else. Part of the reasoning behind this focus was due to economic trade. There was also the fear that the Moroccan forces might aggressively swoop down on vulnerable northern frontiers of the Mali Empire as well.

In fact, centuries later, it would be Moroccan military adventurism that would eventually rip important previously Malian-controlled trade cities, such as Timbuktu and Gao, from the Malian orbit for good. Having said that, as shrewd of a ruler as Mansa Musa was, he knew how important securing his northern frontiers were, so he knew that this meant being able to deal with the Mali Empire's northern neighbor, Morocco, on a friendly basis. And in his efforts of dealing with the Moroccans, Mansa Musa was willing to send his emissaries to sultans as well as common, everyday local traders if he felt it would help him keep an ear to the ground to the rumblings of Moroccan ambition.

It was shortly after this consultation with the local traders that Mansa Musa and his entourage once again picked up and began to trek across the desert. Their next stop would be the town of Ghat in Libya. After passing through Ghat, the instances of human habitation would become fewer and farther between.

During this period, it was much easier for doubts and disagreements to surface, and it has been recorded that the mansa's court had to convene to settle arbitrary matters much more frequently during this stage of the journey. Nevertheless, the general impetus to reach Mecca was never in question, and whatever petty disagreements arose, they were eventually settled. In these instances, Mansa Musa played the role of the ultimate arbitrator, and he attempted to be as light-handed as he could when dealing with the problems of his people.

It is said that when Mansa Musa was pushed by some of his advisors to take a firmer hand with some of his more disagreeable subjects, he took it all in stride and instead quoted from scripture, "He who makes the pilgrimage neither cohabits nor errs—nor contests during his pilgrimage. Here, Allah loves peace makers." As one can see, Mansa Musa sought to present himself as a great peacemaker as he traversed across the vast desert sands of North Africa.

In truth, to keep the cohesion of his traveling party, Mansa Musa would need all of the peacemaking and diplomatic skills at his disposal. This was demonstrated later on the journey when a very startling bit of bad luck befell Mansa Musa's caravan. They were out on the open road again when several members of Mansa Musa's party were inflicted by snake bites. Such things can certainly be deadly out in the open desert, and perhaps even worse than the few who might perish is the threat of fear and panic that such an event can spread through the ranks.

It is said that those who were bitten were in horrible condition, screaming and writhing on the ground as the venom coursed through their body. Court physicians tried their best to treat the injured with traditional remedies, such as applying goat milk and cutting open the wounds with knives that had been heated up in the fire. But unfortunately, this age-old method of cleansing snake bites seemed to have very little effect. And as those stricken worsened, with some even perishing, the fears of the whole group increased.

Soon, there were whispers that snakes had infested the whole caravan and were even holed up in the bags of food and other items the group carried with them. If one so much as opened a bag of grain, there would have been a fear that a snake could suddenly spring forth and strike the hand unfortunate enough to have opened it. In such a fearful environment, snakes were everywhere. Sticks became snakes, ropes were pythons, and even a sudden play of shadows across the desert seemed to become venomous vipers ready to strike.

Wild gossip began to circulate that the whole desert might be impassable due to the snakes. And soon, some even openly spoke of turning back. For those familiar with scripture, this series of events almost seems to parallel the biblical story of **Moses** in the desert with the children of Israel. In this account, Moses's followers were suddenly waylaid by snakes after bitterly complaining that they wished to turn back.

Considering the similarity, it is indeed somewhat ironic that **Mansa Musa**, whose very name "Musa" is the Arabic form of **Moses**, faced just such a dilemma. But that is not to say that the event did not occur or was somehow borrowed from scripture. After all, getting bit by a snake in the desert is a common enough occurrence, and it could happen to just about anyone.

At any rate, in such a climate of fear, it took all of Mansa Musa's skills as a leader to keep his entire group from disintegrating into absolute chaos. According to lore, just as discipline was about to break down entirely, Musa received unexpected aid from a man who had tagged along with the caravan from one of their previous stops. The young man claimed to be knowledgeable in the arts of healing and had a plan to save those dying from the snake bites. He instructed the king to slaughter twelve camels, to cut their stomachs open, and to place the feet and hands of those bitten by the snakes into a camel's belly. All of this was done while those in attendance were directed to repeatedly chant certain passages from the Quran. At first glance, such a thing might seem to be simple superstition. And indeed, the solution employed by the shaman incorporated ancestral beliefs and folk remedies, with Islamic flourishes thrown into the mix. However, it has been said that what this man directed to have done to the injured saved their lives.

Despite the strange theatrics involved, the act of putting wounded limbs into the belly of the camel caused the digestive fluid inside the camel's stomach to react to the venom in the wounds of those stricken. The stomach acid inside the camel's digestive system was able to break down the poison, and after a few hours of being given this treatment, most were able to recover.

It certainly must not have been a pretty sight to see several snakebite victims with their hands and feet stuffed into the bellies of dead camels. But if it had the effect of saving their lives, it was most certainly worth it. This ingenious treatment not only saved the lives of those who had been bitten, but it also no doubt prevented a wider panic—and ultimately dissension—from breaking out in the ranks.

It is said that Mansa Musa was incredibly impressed with the young stranger's knowledge, and from that day forward, he was a trusted member of Musa's court. Even during a great journey such as this, if one was able to prove themselves worthy, Mansa Musa was more than willing to make them a part of his inner circle.

One such subject who proved herself worthy of Mansa Musa's esteem was a slave that he had previously procured who originally hailed as far afield as Baghdad. Not much is known about this young woman—even her very name seems to have been forgotten—but it is said that she was Mansa Musa's favorite among all of his female servants. The more cynical might be inclined to think that the reasoning behind this favoritism might be due to simple physical attraction. The woman was indeed described as being beautiful, but Mansa Musa's affection for her was not only skin-deep. Mansa Musa respected her as a trusted advisor and especially appreciated her ability to recite poetry and verses from the Quran. He also enjoyed the fact that she was from the very heart of the Islamic world, and he depended upon her to fill him in on cultural and ideological issues that he did not understand.

But after Mansa Musa's favorite recited a poem at one of the ruler's dinner parties, the esteem with which she was held began to provoke Mansa Musa's other servants to jealousy. As a result, they began to speak badly about the girl from Baghdad. They spoke angrily of the fact that the mansa was spending so much time with a foreigner and even voiced concern that perhaps state secrets might be passed from Mansa Musa to this exotic slave girl, believing she might be a potential spy. Those concerned that the emperor had been compromised didn't have to worry long, however, because the girl was soon afflicted with a terrible fever and died.

Feverish outbreaks of sickness had been periodically running through the camp for a while, and once one of those viral strains reached the girl from Baghdad, her immune system proved incapable of fending it off. The progress of the caravan was momentarily stopped so that the mansa—in his great sadness—could bury his favorite servant. As her funeral rites commenced, the ruler was remembered to have remarked on just how grieved he felt to know that he would never be able to speak to his special friend again.

Since the Malian emperor was generally supposed to be detached from his subjects, this must have been quite an amazing sight for the Malians to see. The emperor typically presented himself in a stoic, if not slightly cold, fashion. The people were not used to their ruler showing outward emotion or even much outward affection at all, and here he was, pouring his heart out over the body of his dead servant.

Mansa Musa had his court dig a grave for the girl right there in the Sahara Desert, and with her body wrapped in the leaves from a palm tree, she was put into the ground and laid to rest. It is said that she was set down on her side so that she was facing Mecca. Even though she wouldn't survive the journey to the holy city, she would eternally rest with her face toward it.

Chapter 6 – In the Land of Egypt

"There is no need for a traveler on the Nile to take any provision with him, because whenever he wishes to descend on the bank he may do so, for ablutions, prayers, purchasing provisions, or any other purpose. There is a continuous series of bazaars from the city of Alexandria to Cairo. Cities and villages succeed one another along its banks without interruption and have no equal in the inhabited world, nor is any river known whose basin is so intensively cultivated as that of the Nile. There is no river on Earth but it which is called a sea."

-Ibn Battuta

After a long journey in the desert, Mansa Musa and his entourage finally reached the land of Egypt, where they set up camp just outside of the famed pyramids. They waited here until an official sent by Al-Nasir Muhammad, the Sultan of Egypt and Syria, came to officially invite the Malian emperor to have an audience with the sultan at his palace. This visit by the sultan's envoy was, of course, followed by the customary round of gift-giving.

In the Arab world, hospitality between a host and their prospective guests is considered sacrosanct. It is said that this notion of a heavy emphasis on meeting the needs of visitors harkens back to ancient times when it was considered one's duty to aid those traveling through the harsh desert terrain. This was done in the hopes that one would similarly be honored when they themselves were in the same predicament.

For a weary traveler who may not have enough food or even water to last them for the duration of their journey, the idea that they could depend on local hospitality to help them through their ordeal was not only a nicety but an actual necessity. This common aid among desert dwellers soon morphed into a complex ritual of hosts meeting the needs of their guests, which can still be seen in Arab households to this very day.

Upon his arrival in Cairo, Egypt, Mansa Musa, as a visiting king, was immediately considered the personal guest of the sultan, and he was endowed with gifts and amenities considered worthy of a man of his station. He was given a grand copy of the Quran with brilliantly illuminated pages, with blue, red, and gold lettering. He was also gifted with a couple of grand chandeliers for his palace back home and a set of special glass bottles with inscriptions from the Quran, among other things.

These gifts were then generously reciprocated by Mansa Musa, as he gave the sultan plenty of gold and other priceless treasures. But Mansa Musa didn't end there. Along with giving gifts to the Egyptian sultan, Mansa Musa decided that he wanted to bestow gifts upon the general populace of Egypt as well. In what seems like some ancient humanitarian mission, the great Malian emperor arranged to have gifts of clothes and food distributed to the poor and homeless masses who lived on Cairo's streets.

The fact that Mansa Musa would engage in such a humanitarian act shows that he not only knew the plight of the poor in Egypt in advance but that he was also willing to do something about it. This was a fact that was surely not forgotten among the thankful recipients, who were given more aid by this visiting stranger than they had ever been given from their own potentate, the sultan.

Such a great act of random kindness would be something like billionaire Bill Gates suddenly popping up on the southside of Chicago and handing out thousands of dollars at a time to all the folks who sleep under bridges and call back alley dumpsters home. This golden bedecked Malian emperor seeking out Egypt's down and out just to hand them fistfuls of gold must have truly been a sight to behold.

As it pertained to the diplomatic front, after a few more back-and-forth dialogues between representatives of Mansa Musa and the sultan, Mansa Musa was invited to come to the palace before the upcoming Friday prayer. Mansa Musa initially tried to get out of making an appearance, stating that he was traveling through the region for purely religious reasons and did not want to have to create any unnecessary commotion by having the sultan play host for him and his entourage. But along with the age-old excuse of a guest not wanting to put a host out, there was another reason that Mansa Musa did not want to visit the sultan. He knew that it was the custom of those paying respect to the sultan to kneel before him on the ground. Mansa Musa, being a great king and not willing to bow to any other man, did not wish to do this out of principle. Yet, as a guest of the sultan, certain court customs were expected to be observed. This was the dilemma that Mansa Musa faced.

However, as Sultan Al-Nasir Muhammad's officials kept pestering Musa to see the sultan, Mansa Musa came up with a plan. He was going to bow to the earth when he was before the sultan, but he was going to do so as he loudly gave thanks to God, thereby showing that he was not bowing to the sultan as much as he was bowing to God. This may seem like a bit of somersaulting semantics here, but for Mansa Musa, the difference was important, and he saw it as the only way he could go and meet with the sultan.

Once this was decided, Mansa Musa then took select members of his entourage with him to go to the sultan's court. This group was met and flanked by the sultan's guardsmen, who escorted them to the king's palace. The denizens of Cairo gathered in the streets to witness the grand procession. They were amazed to see this man from Mali, sitting astride a majestic, white horse, wearing a fine fur cloak with golden embroidery and a silken turban, inlaid with diamonds and gems.

Mansa Musa and his entourage arrived in the courtyard of the palace before being led up to the personal chambers of the sultan himself. Upon seeing Mansa Musa, the sultan, who was seated on his throne, stood up and began to walk toward the emperor of Mali. Mansa Musa then kneeled down on the floor, and as planned, he loudly declared in Arabic, "I prostrate myself before Allah, who created me and brought me into this world," making it clear to everyone within earshot that he was not prostrating himself before the sultan but rather God himself. The sultan then offered the hearty rejoinder, "Allah is great! And Muhammad is his prophet!" After these things were said, the two men greeted each other, and then Sultan Al-Nasir Muhammad led Mansa Musa to sit right beside him as an equal.

Even though they sat right next to each other, the two men usually did not speak directly to one another. Instead, Mansa Musa spoke to the sultan through his translator. This was not so much because Mansa Musa's Arabic was rusty; by all accounts, he was quite fluent. It was simply done out of tradition. Mansa Musa always spoke through his translator when he held court at home, and he continued to do so while he held court abroad. This practice later caused some friction with certain dignitaries who found it insulting, but it was simply a part of Mansa Musa's normal protocol.

At any rate, through this court official, the sultan learned that Mali was indeed a rich realm of abundance. The sultan was informed of the massive gold deposits, salt mines, and the great forests that produced valuable timber. The sultan was also intrigued to know that Islam was rapidly growing in West Africa. Mansa Musa, in the meantime, expressed through his translator his admiration of Cairo's many monuments and mosques. He especially appreciated the ornate stained glass windows, which apparently had just been installed in many of the main mosques recently. To these compliments, Sultan Al-Nasir Muhammad is said to have replied at length:

My brother, your words touch me profoundly. Indeed, our works and those of our predecessors exist only for the glory of our Lord and the well-being of our subjects accordingly to the dictates of the Prophet. I also know the extent of your works, the multiplication of the houses of God on your travels to Timbuktu, to Doukourei, to Goudam, to Dierei, to Quanko to Bako, your generosity toward the peoples you met along your route, your care for the most destitute as instructed by the Prophet. It is our intention to remake our city. These works are made possible by the peace which reigns in the Empire, all the way to the far-off lands of India where our cousin, the Mameluke Sultan of Delhi, reigns. The prosperity of these times follows a long period of penury, of food shortage, and epidemics; our present political stability follows a painful succession of coups and usurpations of which many were extremely violent. I myself was forced to cede power on two occasions. The poem of Ibn Mougha, the father of our literature, born in Baghdad, expresses beautifully what I underwent then: "Fortune frowned on me for a half-day: no more was needed for my friend to flee, putting as much distance as possible between themselves and me." Those days are over. Peace at home and peace abroad are henceforth one. Tolerance is shown to all religious minorities and foreigners who keep their own system of justice for the management of their own internal affairs, but our justice is the same for all. The special laws which applied to them have been abolished. We are at pains to mete out justice personally twice weekly.

We hear the plea, question the plaintiffs and rule by seeking to approach the fairness of God. Our Capital speaks every language of the world, some people believe that the genius of man is unlimited and that his achievements are and will be as well. These people are blasphemers! The highways from Byzantium to Mecca, from Tripoli to Tabriz, from Grenada to Jerusalem are all secure.

These words must be taken with a large grain of salt (perhaps one of the largest grains ever to have been extracted from one of Mali's salt mines) since historians know full well just how dangerous travel was in those days. After all, if the roads were really that secure, pilgrims on the hajj would not have had to constantly worry about being ambushed by bandits along the way. Even Mansa Musa, with his vast entourage that included thousands of troops, eventually became susceptible to this very sort of predation. Anyone who strayed away from the main group was likely to be snatched up like stray sheep by wolves on the prowl.

To be clear, this is by no means hyperbole on the part of this writer. Even the Arab scholar Ibn Khaldun readily recorded how, when Mansa Musa eventually began his return trip from Mecca, part of Mansa Musa's caravan got cut off from the main group, and many were kidnapped and even enslaved by Bedouin raiders. But we will discuss this matter in depth a little later in this book.

After their dialogue came to an end, Sultan Al-Nasir Muhammad informed Mansa Musa that he had a whole palace prepared for him near the Mameluke tombs, located in the vicinity of Mount Moggataru. He was also informed that as soon as he and his companions had rested enough, restocked their provisions, and were ready to resume their pilgrimage, he would have his officials help to protect and guide their caravan to Mecca. From his perch at his new palace in Cairo, Mansa Musa temporarily became an additional head of state in Egypt next to the sultan himself.

And as a head of state, Mansa Musa held court and received dignitaries. It was in this capacity that he held an audience with the Abbasid calif of Baghdad. With him, Mansa Musa discussed many aspects of Islamic ideology as well as general philosophies of life. Mansa Musa was also keenly interested in the latest developments in science and mathematics. After all, during this period, Egypt was a great center of learning when it came to both.

The Islamic world had inherited advanced concepts from both Greece and India, and Arab scholars had perfected these concepts even further. The Arabs borrowed the idea of numerals (1,2,3,4) from India, for example, but were able to streamline their use with the creation of new mathematical systems, such as algebra. The name "algebra" itself comes from Arabic.

As anyone who has studied Arabic knows, the word "al" is the Arab equivalent of "the." Al-Jazeera, a popular news program broadcast from the Arab world, for example, means "The Island," which is in reference to Qatar, where the news station first took root. It should be noted that Qatar is technically a peninsula and not an island, though. Another example that's much more infamous would be the terrorist group Al-Qaeda, which translates as "The Base."

Having said that, one might easily conclude that "Al-Gebra" might simply mean "The Math." But as neat and tidy as that might sound, that is not the case. "Al-Gebra," roughly translated, is a phrase that means "The reunion of broken parts." And if you think of what algebra actually does, with all of its formulas and equations that seek to find solutions by plugging in various variables, it is indeed a reunion of broken parts.

Mansa Musa, who was a lifelong scholar, was quite fascinated with all of these aspects of higher learning available to him in Cairo. And considering all of the purchases he was making in Egypt, it was probably a good thing that he learned a little math along the way.

During his stay in Cairo, Mansa Musa engaged in spent much money buying supplies and provisions. Among the more expensive items were extravagant book covers for the Quran, composed of fine materials such as lace and ebony; prayer rugs; and painted glass showcasing brightly illuminated passages from the Quran. Mansa Musa also regularly sent court officials out to the major shopping bazaars in Egypt to get plenty of fine spices, such as myrrh, camphor, and nutmeg, some of it coming as far afield as Indonesia in Southeast Asia.

Some of the other more extravagant items that Mansa Musa purchased were a few magnetic compasses that had been made in China. The compass was still a fairly novel invention, and the idea that a traveler who had one in their possession would always be able to make their way north (at least magnetic north) was a real confidence booster for any journey. With such equipment, at least some fear of ending up completely lost during a sandstorm in the desert could be somewhat alleviated.

Incredibly enough, by the time Mansa Musa was through shelling out gold (all of his purchases were made in raw gold pieces) in Egypt, he managed to crash the whole gold market in the region. This was caused not just by his purchases but also by his generous donations of gold. It is said that Mansa Musa managed to put a dent in the overall value of gold in Egypt by as much as 25 percent.

Part of this massive influx was brought on by greedy Egyptians, as the sellers routinely marked up their wares, hoping that the rich would pay more for much less. And for the most part, Mansa Musa did just that, often paying five times as much for an item than it was actually worth.

Although Mansa Musa tended to turn a blind eye to this price gouging, many of those traveling with him took note, and it has been said that this unfair treatment was remembered long after Mansa Musa and his court returned to Mali. The memory of this offense, which has been recorded in Malian lore, as well as the actual Egyptian records of Mansa Musa's heavy use of gold, which crashed the Egyptian economy, certainly paints an interesting picture.

Even more interesting perhaps have been the subsequent theories proposed to offer an alternate explanation as to what Mansa Musa might have really been up to. It has long been suggested that it was Mansa Musa's innocent, almost child-like generosity that inadvertently crashed Cairo's economy. Other historians, however, beg to differ. Citing the fact that Mansa Musa was a highly intelligent and even shrewd politician, some have theorized that Mansa Musa knew exactly what he was doing.

According to this line of thought, Mansa Musa might not have been as kindhearted as we believe and that he actually crashed Egypt's economy on purpose! Why would Mansa Musa do such a thing? Well, as it turns out, Egypt was a direct competitor in the gold markets at the time, and by exerting control over it—by way of flooding its markets with excess gold—Mansa Musa was able to take out an economic rival. And while doing so, he appeared to be completely blameless, as he played these acts off as an extraordinarily generous gesture of a great king.

If this was indeed Mansa Musa's intentions, his crafty scheme worked like a charm. Egypt's economy took several years to recover, and Mali's gold markets continued to dominate the world. And in the meantime, Mansa Musa's famous "generosity" cemented him as an international legend. Is this why there appears to be a knowing smirk on Mansa Musa's portrait on the Catalan Atlas? One can only wonder.

Chapter 7 – Mansa Resumes His Pilgrimage

"The people fasted for three successive days, the last of which was a Thursday. At the end of this period, the amirs, sharifs, qadis, doctors of the Law, and all other classes of the people in their several degrees, assembled in the Great mosque, until it was filled to overflowing with them, and spent Thursday night there in prayers and liturgies and supplications. Then, after performing the dawn prayer—they all went out together on foot carrying Qurans in their hands—the amirs too, barefooted. The entire population of the city joined in the exodus, male and female, small and large, the Jews went out with their book and the law and the Christians with their Gospel, their women and children with them; the whole concourse of them in tears and humble supplications, imploring the favor of God through his books and his prophets."

-Ibn Battuta

Mansa Musa and his court left Cairo as the Egyptian summer turned to fall, staying for about three months in total. Mansa Musa left with just about as much fanfare as with which he had arrived, and the Egyptian people would not soon forget him. Mansa Musa and his companions soon crossed the Red Sea and entered Saudi Arabia itself. The sultan of Egypt had called ahead of his guest and made sure that special depots with additional provisions would be set up along the way.

The sultan had also made sure that military leaders in the region were aware that the pilgrimage was taking place and put out instructions that the pilgrims be carefully looked after. Compared to the struggle of crossing the Sahara Desert in North Africa, this well-provisioned and well-attended last leg of the journey was much easier. Before reaching Mecca, Mansa Musa and company made a stop in Medina, the town in which the Prophet Muhammad's mortal remains rest.

Here, Mansa Musa visited the fabled Green Mosque, where both the prophet and a couple of the original caliphs—Abu Bakr and Umar—were entombed. It was shortly after Mansa Musa paid his respects in Medina that the caravan was able to make it to the outskirts of the Saudi Arabian city of Mecca—the main focal point of all of Islam. As Mansa Musa's entourage approached, it was, once again, quite a spectacle for the locals to behold.

Mansa Musa's mobile palace was a grand tent encampment, as Mansa Musa's kingly tent was flanked by thousands of other tents for his followers. There were also countless pack animals carrying all manner of provisions, as well as gifts both received and those yet to be given. Mansa Musa's own generosity when it came to gift-giving was quite well known by then.

Upon entering the city of Mecca, each one of these visitors had to buy a special pass or "visa" in order to enter the city. These passes worked much like a modern-day visa, allowing travelers to have temporary official permission to remain in the region. Once this was acquired, the pilgrims could pass freely into the great city of Mecca. During this procession, some rode on the backs of camels, but many more walked on their own two feet.

Mecca was an impressive sight to see in those days, but even before the rise of Islam, the city of Mecca was a major hub in the region. Mecca served as a trading outpost for various neighboring regions, such as Yemen, Ethiopia, Syria, the Byzantine Empire, and even far-away India.

As Mansa Musa and his fellow pilgrims made their way through Mecca, they made sure to follow all of the traditional rules and rituals that were expected of pilgrims as they approached the Great Mosque of Mecca, which houses the religious shrine of the Kaaba. The hajj itself is supposed to demonstrate the solidarity of Muslims in their reverence of God as they march in lockstep to the Kaaba, which is considered to represent "Bayt Allah," or as it would be in English, the "House of God."

It is not so much that Muslims literally believe that God calls the forty-three-foot-high, thirty-six-foot-wide cube-shaped structure home as much as it represents the presence of God to the Muslim faithful. And as Mansa Musa made his way to the structure, he was no doubt in the company of countless devout Muslims from all over the Islamic world.

Once inside the Great Mosque, Mansa Musa and those with him would have walked around the Kaaba seven times in a counter-clockwise direction. Although the ritual is mainly done in commemoration of Muhammad's supposed final journey from the site of the Kaaba to the Al-Aqsa Mosque in Jerusalem and then on to heaven, it is believed that the tradition dates back to Abraham.

Abraham is said to have visited the valley of Mecca, where his son, Ishmael, had been taken in prior years by the handmaiden whom Abraham had impregnated—Hagar. According to Islamic lore, the archangel Gabriel, who helped guide Ishmael and his mother Hagar through the desert, gave the child a black rock, which then ended up inside the Kaaba. A black stone still resides in the Kaaba to this day, which visitors touch to receive a blessing. Some believe that the rock is actually part of a meteorite.

In pre-Islamic times, when the locals were primarily polytheists who worshiped a wide variety of deities, the structure of the Kaaba was actually a shelter in which various stone idols were stored for a multiplicity of local religious practices. In that sense, it is somewhat ironic that Muhammad would eventually consecrate the shrine for Islam, as the religion is steadfastly against idolatry.

At any rate, as it pertains to Mansa Musa, his pilgrimage was filled with many moments of surprise and discovery. During his hajj, he made more of the big purchases he had become famous for, buying a couple hundred prayer rugs, as well as 150 religious manuscripts, all paid with, once again, a vast amount of gold. In all, Mansa Musa's pilgrimage in Mecca lasted for twelve days. During this time, he made sure to wear the all-white, spotless garments of a pilgrim. He also made sure to take off his flashy gold and jewels and put them to the side before he neared the Kaaba since a pilgrim on the hajj—even a powerful king such as Mansa Musa—is expected to be modest.

It was in this garb that Mansa Musa entered the great mosque, touched the black stone, drank from precious fountains, bowed to the ground in prayer, and circled the Kaaba in the procession of faithful believers. After taking part in the procession around the Kaaba, Mansa Musa ended up staying in the city of Mecca for a few more months. So, while the pilgrimage itself lasted for twelve days, Mansa Musa stayed on as a visitor to the city a few months after that.

During this time, Mansa Musa embarked upon a campaign to get the Meccan authorities to allow him to bring a few "descendants" of Muhammad back with him. In Islam, especially in ancient times, men who could claim descendance from Muhammad were revered as devout teachers of Islam. And Mansa Musa wanted to bring a few of them back to his realm so that they could help better instill Islamic tradition in the Mali Empire. Initially, the grand sharif, who was in charge of such matters, refused to allow any such thing. It took some time and a bit of a pressure campaign on the part of Mansa Musa's diplomatic representatives, but finally, the Meccan authorities relented and decreed that if one of the descendants wished to travel with Mansa Musa, they would be permitted to do so.

Once this permission was granted, Mansa Musa made sure to create as much incentive as possible. He had it announced that he would hand out a small fortune in gold to any descendant of Muhammad who would make the journey with him back to Mali. Due to his generosity, he ended up having four descendants of Muhammad agree to join his caravan. He also met a lot of other interesting people, including a famed architect from Spanish Granada named Abu-Ishaq Ibrahim-es-Saheli. This architect would actually be convinced to travel back to Mali with Mansa Musa's entourage, and upon his arrival to the Mali Empire, he was commissioned to build several grand mosques and other structures and monuments. The Spanish Muslim would use techniques that blended both classic European and Arab design, as well as unique and astonishing innovations that were all his own.

Upon his return home, Mansa Musa was proud that he was now an official hajji, and he was determined to bring back as much of the wonder he had experienced to his own homeland. But before he sent his caravan back toward Mali, he had a special private meeting with his most trusted griot to record some very important thoughts that had intruded upon his mind.

As the griot sat and listened to what his sovereign had to say, Mansa Musa reported, "I should carry myself before you like the happiest man in the world. We have crossed half the world without a major trial, apart from the death of my favorite slave [the woman from Baghdad] and the loss of a score of our companions. We have been received everywhere according to our station, welcomed, supported, and protected. We have seen, in the latter regard, how other sovereigns act, their traditions and their works. As you so love to say: In due time, we will do as the bees, making the same honey from many different flowers. We have acquired objects of great import for the material and spiritual well-being of our subjects. During our absence, our kingdom has known peace and prosperity."

After Mansa Musa continued at some length about all of the accomplishments that had been achieved, the old griot gave his own forecast of what the future might hold. The griot declared, "Our sons and the sons of our sons and their sons will know terrible times. They will be forced outside of the equality of all men. But no matter where they are, they will retain in their hearts and in their minds the hope born of your long voyage, and of all you have evoked, such as your reception according to your rank. Where ever they may be, they will keep in their hearts and in their minds the hope born of your pilgrimage."

Some have interpreted these sayings to be a kind of prophecy of things to come. It could be seen as an interpretation of a time in the future in which Mali would be subjugated and brought under the yoke of foreign oppression. And this would indeed happen to Mali in the centuries to come, as enemies from abroad would take advantage of an increasingly splintered Malian civilization.

In that sense, it seems that the old griot was prophesying to Mansa Musa that even in those dark days ahead, Malians will always look back at the days of greatness under his reign and be proud. As the griot contends, wherever Malians may be, no matter where their diaspora may take them, they will always look back on the epic pilgrimage that Mansa Musa made, and their hearts and minds will be filled with hope for their future and immense pride for their past.

Chapter 8 – Heading Back Home

"We kissed the holy stone; we performed a prayer of two bowings at the Maqam Ibrahim and clung to the curtains of the Kaaba at the Multazam between the door and the black stone, where prayer is answered; we drank of the water of Zamzam. Then having run between al-Safa and al-Marwa, we took up our lodging there in a house near the Gate of Ibrahim."

-Ibn Battuta

Mansa Musa may have been the richest man in the world, but by the time he got back to Cairo, Egypt, he was flat broke. It had been a rough trip between Mecca and Cairo, and at one point, Mansa Musa and his core group of followers became separated from the rest. They ended up being so lost that even Mansa Musa's Chinese compasses failed to regain their bearings.

Caught in a sandstorm in the middle of the desert, one becomes quite easily disoriented. Mansa Musa and his fellow lost companions ended up making their way out to the Suez (the later site of the Suez Canal). Here, they were able to survive on whatever they could fish out of the waters, but the situation was downright grim. There were bandits lurking everywhere, waiting to strike weary, worn-out, and lost travelers just like Mansa Musa and his entourage. Anyone who lingered too far from the pack was indeed ambushed and forced into slavery.

Just imagine being out fishing for some food for your dinner only to have a Bedouin charge at you, tie you up, and throw you on the back of a camel. It certainly wasn't much fun for those who were captured, that's for sure. Fortunately for many of these hapless victims of the Bedouin, the name and fame of Mansa Musa were enough to gain the release of many. But even for those who were not kidnapped, the threat of dying out on the desert would claim many.

Mansa Musa needed more cash in order to continue provisioning his caravan for the journey home to Mali, so he resorted to taking out loans from Egyptian financiers. One of those financiers was a man by the name of Siraj al-Din. Although his pockets were currently empty, Siraj knew that Mansa Musa had more than enough money waiting for him back home. Even so, in order to ensure that Mansa Musa would make good on paying back the money he had lent, he arranged to have one of his own representatives (or some would say bill collectors) join Mansa Musa's entourage for the trip back to Mali. However, as it turned out, Siraj al-Din's loan officer got cold feet and backed out at the last minute. This left Siraj al-Din with the choice of either fully putting his trust into the Malian emperor to keep his word and repay him or to go along for the ride himself. Siraj al-Din was a crafty businessman, and he wasn't about to leave his repayment to fate, so he ended up joining the caravan and traveling back to Mali with the monarch himself.

He also made the decision to have his son join him on the journey. It would later prove wise that he did so since Siraj al-Din died during the trip. Some would later speculate that the money broker was poisoned. But the motive for such an act remains unclear. Mansa Musa himself certainly would not have had the man killed, as this would have been completely out of character for him. It also would not make much sense since Mansa Musa had more than enough money back home to repay the broker.

At any rate, since Siraj al-Din's son had come along for the journey, he was more than able to collect on his father's behalf. It was also Siraj al-Din's son who helped to squelch rumors that his father had been assassinated. Siraj al-Din's son insisted that his father's death was a natural one, reminding those who jumped to conclusions that he had dined on the same portions of supposed poisoned fare that his father had, yet he was none the worse for wear. In the end, this son would be able to finish the journey to Mali, and he would be given what his father had been owed in full, proving that Mansa Musa had no reason to cause any harm.

The death of Siraj al-Din caused much unwarranted drama, but Mansa Musa was also in for some good news too. On his way back home, he received the astonishing tidings that his great general, Sagamandia, had not only put down an insurgency in the region of Gao but that he had also managed to completely annex Gao to the Mali Empire.

Mansa Musa was delighted at the news, and he would later begin several building projects in the region, including the great Gao Mosque, which can still be visited this very day. This mosque serves as a lasting testament to the greatness of his rule, as do other structures that were erected by Mansa Musa. Mansa Musa had a reach that extended far and wide, and his fame reached the ears of all who resided within the boundaries of his sprawling dominion.

Gao, which had long been a rich and prosperous region due to its abundance of copper and salt, was a real boon to Mansa Musa. Gao was actually founded by fishermen in the 7th century, and it went on to become one of the greatest centers of trade in West Africa. Gao then became the capital city of the thriving Songhai Empire in the early 1000s. Under Songhai dominion, the city of Gao was a thriving outpost, trading copper, gold, salt, and even slaves.

The region was strategically and geographically important, as it controlled a major portion of the Niger River. It was also a kind of breadbasket since the land was fertile, and there was also a rich capacity for agriculture. Mansa Musa, who was elated to hear of these developments, decided to make an immediate detour on his journey back to the Malian capital and made his way directly to Gao instead. He planned to meet with the recently deposed king of Gao and affirm his leadership over the region. He also had intentions of taking the king's two princely sons as "hostages."

As hostile or even downright criminal as such an act might sound today, the taking of royal hostages was actually a common practice in those days. A royal hostage was taken from a deposed potentate in order to ensure the deposed leader's future cooperation. It was kind of an insurance policy that would prevent the defeated party from doing anything rash while the conquering authorities were away. Royal hostages were always well taken care of, but they were still technically prisoners in gilded cages, used for the purpose of ensuring stability in recently annexed territories.

On his way to Gao, Mansa Musa made a pitstop at the city of Ghadames. This settlement was located in modern-day Libya, and it boasted a Roman fortress dating back several centuries. Here, it is said that Mansa Musa met an interesting character, a desert commander who was engaged in guerilla raids against enemy tribes in the region of Wargala (also spelled as Ouargla). This renegade apparently sought an audience with the Malian emperor to see if he would be interested in assisting his war efforts against Wargala. The official lore grows silent as to what—if anything—came of such war plans. The guerilla commander, however, is remembered as having left Ghadames to journey on with Mansa Musa to the region of Gao.

At any rate, when Mansa Musa arrived at the gates of Gao, he was greeted by the king, who agreed to hand over his two princely sons—Suleiman Nar and Ali Kolon—as royal hostages. Even with the loss of Gao, the Songhai Empire carried on, and it would wait in the wings for its chance to reclaim lost ground.

As important as Gao may have been, it was the capture of Timbuktu that would prove the most pivotal. At the time, Timbuktu was only second in importance for the Songhai Empire, with Gao as the most important, but Mansa Musa would come to make Timbuktu eclipse and ultimately surpass Gao in many ways. Mansa Musa renovated the city and allowed it to become a major trading hub and weigh station between several North African trade routes, connecting places such as Fez, Morocco, and Cairo, Egypt, to towns such as Tuat and Ghadames.

But as important to trade as Timbuktu would become, Mansa Musa also made it a focal point for education. He installed several mosques, universities, and other cultural centers in the city. Mansa Musa turned Timbuktu into a vast repository for all of the wonderful things that he had learned during his hajj. It was Mansa Musa, after all, who installed the Sankore center of learning, which would later lead to the University of Sankore.

These institutions would not only serve as learning centers for those who lived in the region but also for any Islamic scholars willing to make the trek and learn abroad. And as the renown of the institutions grew, many would indeed become willing to make that journey. Mansa Musa put Abu-Ishaq Ibrahim-es-Saheli—the Grenadian architect who had chosen to come to the Mali Empire with Musa—to work over the next few years, building all kinds of mosques, memorials, and institutions of learning in Timbuktu and Gao.

Many of these are now considered World Heritage Sites, and in 1990, the city of Timbuktu itself ended up on the World Heritage List of Endangered Places, courtesy of UNESCO (United Nations Educational, Scientific and Cultural Organization). Unfortunately, several were vandalized, and some were completely destroyed in the 2010s by radical Islamic extremists. Three of the so-called "sacred tombs," which belonged to past Malian leaders—Sidi Mahmoud, Sidi Moctar, and Alpha Moya—were some of the sites completely destroyed by the looters.

The most important work that Abu-Ishaq Ibrahim-es-Saheli constructed in Timbuktu was the Djinguereber Mosque, which was completed in 1327. The structure is quite unique because it has a framework of wooden timber that protrudes out of the walls. The desert terrain of Timbuktu often makes for a dynamic and even unusual setting, and these unique structures, with wooden planks sticking out of them like some kind of desert porcupines, further adds to the otherworldly experience.

Another great building project that was commissioned during this period was a palace called the Madugu, which would be Mansa Musa's home away from home when visiting the city. It is said that Abu-Ishaq Ibrahim-es-Saheli received a handsome amount of gold for his efforts.

Once Mansa Musa set these great things in motion, he finally began to prepare for the journey back to the capital of the Mali Empire—Niani. Mansa Musa opted to put many of the women, as well as some of the Islamic scholars who had traveled with him, on boats to sail down the local Niger River, while Mansa Musa and the main contingent would continue back to the capital overland. This decision would cause some unexpected drama when Dian, which was a vassal state of Mali at the time, attacked the ships as they sailed past. The lord of Dian was apparently planning on taking everyone prisoner, but once he realized just how distinguished his hostages were, he decided to let them go on their way. Mansa Musa and his entourage all safely returned to the capital city with more than their fair share of stories to tell.

Chapter 9 – Return to the Capital

"The people of Mali outnumbered the peoples of the Sudan in their neighborhood and dominated the whole region. Their authority became mighty and all the peoples of the Sudan stood in awe of them."

-Ibn Khaldun

Upon his return to the capital city of Niani, Mansa Musa, fresh off the hajj, was galvanized to strengthen the Islamic influence in his realm. Despite the fact that Mansa Musa was a Muslim and that Islam had more or less become the official state religion, there were still great pockets of resistance to the Muslim faith. Many in his realm still held firm to their ancestral beliefs, and some even openly practiced the dark arts of wizardry and witchcraft.

Such things, of course, are in complete contradiction to Islam. The Quran memorably condemns magic and magicians in its account of Moses facing off against the Egyptian pharaoh's sorcerers. In the Quran, Moses is called "Musa," so it is somewhat ironic that Mansa Musa's namesake is used in one of the Quran's most powerful denunciations of magic. The Quran recounts the biblical story as originally told in Exodus when Moses stood before the pharaoh and his court magicians cast down their rods only for them to transform into snakes. Moses then cast down his staff, and it became an even bigger snake, ostensibly not through magic but through the power of God, allowing Moses (or Musa) to defeat the pharaoh's magicians.

Or as Surah 20:65-70 reports:

They said: Oh Musa! Will you cast, or shall we be the first who cast down? He said: Nay! Cast down. Then lo! Their cords and their rods—it was imaged to him on account of their magic as if they were running. So Musa conceived in his mind a fear. We said: Fear not, surely you shall be the uppermost. And cast down what is in your right hand; it shall devour what they have wrought. They have wrought only the plan of a magician, and the magician shall not be successful wheresoever he may come from. And the magicians were cast down making obeisance; they said: We believe in the Lord of Haroun [Aaron] and Musa [Moses].

As such, Mansa Musa, who had become a dedicated Muslim by this point, was deeply troubled by his own people's resistance in becoming dedicated to the Islamic faith. It seems that many of the hybridized Islamic and pagan practices, which didn't bother Musa before, were troubling to him upon his return. Now, even something as simple as burying one's loved ones created a problem because Mansa Musa had learned the proper last rites that were to be conducted for Muslims, and this tradition was most certainly at odds with what most citizens of the Mali Empire did.

In Mali, the usual custom as it pertained to the burial of the deceased was to have a small funeral service and then simply leave the dead exposed in the bushy wilderness so that nature could take its course. Mansa Musa's Islamic scholars were not too pleased to learn of such things, to say the least. Mansa Musa leaned heavily on the learned men of Islam who had returned home with him, trusting them to instill the religion and culture of what it meant to be a Muslim in his people. He had them institute Islamic prayers on Friday, Islamic dietary laws, social customs, and the like.

Along with making sure that the people were educated about Islam by his Islamic scholars, Mansa Musa also wished to further cement his power by having his favorite architect, Abu-Ishaq Ibrahim-es-Saheli, construct a grand palace for him in Niani. This building would stand out from the rest due to its heavy use of plaster, which was a unique building material in the region at that time. The building was vast, with a special audience hall, courtyard, and other fixtures. The windows stood out for their frames, which were lined in both silver and gold. Abu-Ishaq Ibrahim-es-Saheli was once again handsomely rewarded with his efforts by being given plenty of gold and other gifts and personal perks for the skills that he demonstrated.

Despite all of Mansa Musa's great works, life for the average person in his kingdom remained relatively the same. The average person still continued to live on a diet of mostly rice and a few various fruits and vegetables, and they drank water straight from the local rivers, just as their ancestors before them had done. In the searing Malian heat, most lived in the cool confines of mud dwellings. The mud structures were lined with animal fat, which was also often turned into soap and even used to make torchlights. The biggest, most lasting impact that Mansa Musa had on the lives of the average Malian, however, was the enshrinement of Islam in their hearts. After Mansa Musa returned from his pilgrimage, his efforts of Islamization paid off, and soon, people of all walks of life were attending Friday evening prayer services at their local mosque.

Efforts were also made to study the Quran. Not only that, many attempted to commit the entire Quran to memory, and they instilled this virtue in their children as well. As brutal as it might sound, some parents even put their kids in chains until they had satisfactorily memorized their verses! Arab Scholar Ibn Battuta supposedly witnessed this practice firsthand. He would later recall, "They place fetters on their children if there appears on their part a failure to memorize the Quran, and they are not undone until they memorize it." Call it hands-on parenting or call it horrible abuse, but one thing is for certain—Malian parents were apparently very eager to have their offspring knowledgeable about the Quran. But although Islam became more dominant in the region, some would always hold onto aspects of their ancestral religions. It was also hard for Malians to conform to the more patriarchal structure of Islam.

In Mali, for example, it was common for men and women who were not married to talk with each other freely as equals. Such things, however, were considered anathema to certain tenants of Islam and were not to be permitted. What also most certainly wouldn't have been permitted, at least according to conservative Muslims, was the naked dancing that took place in many traditional festival activities in Mali. Some Muslim visitors, such as Ibn Battuta, took offense to the extravagant demonstrations of ancestral rituals mixed with Islamic practice.

Ibn reported his disgust at seeing "royal poets who romped about in feathers and bird masks," for example, expressing his wish that stricter Islamic protocol be followed in the Mali Empire. Some of Mansa Musa's Islamic scholars who were imported from abroad were indeed quite shocked and horrified to see such practices in place. Mansa Musa, who was undoubtedly embarrassed and concerned that he might lose prestige among his Muslim peers, more than likely cracked down on such excesses as he strengthened the hold of Islam in his kingdom.

Along with making sure that his subjects were educated in Islam, Mansa Musa also wanted to make sure that his own son was equipped to follow in his footsteps after he was gone. Mansa Musa had actually hoped that his son might take over for him even before he died so that he could essentially retire to Saudi Arabia, where he planned to spend his life as a humble monk, renouncing all things of this world. But before he could embark upon any kind of early retirement, Mansa Musa knew that he still had some unfinished business to settle.

By this point, Mansa Musa was quite famous, with whispers of the rich king reaching ears in Italy and Portugal. Soon, these two countries were both competing with Islamic powerbrokers to have access to trade with Mali. Mali's conduct with Portugal actually kicked off the Portuguese desire to explore the west coast of the African continent. But perhaps the most important political alliance that Mansa Musa struck was when he reached out to Abu al-Hasan, who ruled the central Maghreb.

Mansa Musa sent an envoy to the powerful ruler to open up trade relations, and Abu al-Hasan heartily agreed. He knew of Mansa Musa's great reputation and his kingdom's enormous wealth in gold, so he was more than willing to open up a dialogue on trade. He sent the envoys back with both his blessing and several expensive gifts. Mansa Musa, however, would not get to receive them, as he passed away in 1337 before his envoy returned home.

Mansa Musa, like all of us, didn't know the day or the hour of his passing, and he most certainly figured that he had several more years left than he actually did. After all, he was not sick, and by all accounts, his demise was an abrupt and sudden one. And although his son, Mansa Maghan, had filled in for his father in the past and ostensibly had been groomed to succeed him, at this juncture, he seemed a bit unprepared. Being a mansa of such a sprawling empire, after all, is indeed a heavy load to bear. And for whatever reason, Mansa Maghan just no longer seemed up for the challenge. He actually ended up only ruling a few short years before his uncle, Mansa Musa's brother, Mansa Sulayman (also spelled as Suleyman), stepped in to take over.

Chapter 10 – Mali after Mansa Musa

"Whenever a hero adds to the list of his exploits from conquest, Mansa Musa gives them a pair of wide trousers. The greater the number of a Dogari's exploits, the bigger the size of this trousers."

-Al-Dukhari

The Mali Empire was rocked by the news of the great monarch Mansa Musa's abrupt passing in 1337. But as shocking as the loss of this great leader may have been, the Mali Empire initially seemed to be in a good position for a seamless transfer of power since Mansa Musa's son, Maghan, had already been groomed to replace him. But although he had served as an able steward when he filled in for Mansa Musa during his pilgrimage to Mecca, Mansa Maghan proved to be an inept ruler over the long haul.

Unfortunately, or perhaps fortunately considering his ineptitude, after facing a wide variety of problems during his rule, he ended up perishing just a few years later. This occurred around 1341, and that same year, he was replaced on the throne by his own uncle, Sulayman. Sulayman was Mansa Musa's brother, and many hoped that he would prove to be as capable as his sibling when it came to his ability to run the empire.

Mansa Sulayman did show some of the same qualities as his brother in his ability to govern, but he never gained the affection of the public as Mansa Musa did. On the contrary, according to historian David C. Conrad, Mansa Sulayman was not just unpopular but "intensely disliked." There is some indication that Mansa Sulayman was viewed as a usurper even though his placement on the throne would appear to be more a matter of fate than one of political intrigue. It seems the severe dislike that Mansa Sulayman generated among the Malian masses emerged early on, although it is still not entirely clear why Mansa Sulayman struck such a chord with the public. It seems that no matter what this mansa did, his people would always view him as an evil usurper and illegitimate leader.

Nevertheless, whether the people liked him or not, Mansa Sulayman sought to continue right where his brother, Mansa Musa, had left off. It was indeed Sulayman who would establish official relations with Abu al-Hasan of Morocco, just as his late brother Musa had so desired. And Mansa Sulayman, no doubt wishing to show a similar sense of generosity as his deceased brother, held an extravagant welcome party for the first official representatives of Morocco who came to visit.

Unlike Mansa Musa, Mansa Sulayman didn't hesitate to make himself subservient to the sultan, and the Moroccan diplomats went back to Morocco, telling their potentate that Mansa Sulayman was ready to "pay duties" to the sultan and demonstrate his submission. Mansa Sulayman was apparently willing to bow his head if he thought it would gain him a powerful ally.

Mansa Musa, as can be seen in the chapter above when he refused to kneel before the sultan of Cairo (he kneeled to God instead), was not willing to make himself anything other than an equal to his peers on the international stage. Mansa Sulayman had inherited much uncertainty when he came to the throne, however, and he probably figured he could use all the help he could get.

His powerful ally would not remain on the scene for long, though, as a revolution rocked Morocco shortly thereafter. In this popular uprising, Abu al-Hasan was dethroned, captured, and whipped. Many of his troops were killed, and his navy was destroyed. Abu al-Hasan was forced to step down, and his son took over what was left of his father's kingdom. Abu al-Hasan perished in 1351. He was largely disgraced at this point, but his one loyal friend, Mansa Sulayman, held a grand remembrance ceremony in his honor.

Arab scholar Ibn Battuta, who was in Mali for the occasion, vividly recalled the event. He was amazed at both the extravagance and the way in which Islamic and African ancestral traditions merged together. Some elements were similar to what he had observed at countless other Muslim memorials for deceased kings, but other aspects were completely unique to the nature of Mali at this point in history.

As a firsthand eyewitness, Ibn Battuta tells us the following:

[The sultan] has a lofty pavilion, of which the door is inside his house, where he sits from most of the time. There came forth from the gate of the palace about 300 slaves, some carrying in their hands bows and others having in their hands short lances and shields. Then two saddled and bridled horses are brought, with two rams which, they say, are effective against the evil eye. Dugha the interpreter stands at the gate of the council-place wearing fine garments of silk brocade and other materials, and on his head a turban with fringes which they have a novel way of winding. The troops governors, young men, slaves, the Masufa, and others sit outside the council place in a broad street where there are trees. Inside the council place beneath the arches a man is standing. Anyone who wishes to address the sultan addresses Dugha and Dugha addresses that man standing and that man standing addresses the sultan. If one of them addresses the sultan and the latter replies he uncovers the clothes from his back and sprinkles dust on his head and back, like one washing himself with water. I used to marvel how their eyes did not become blinded.

After the death of Abu al-Hasan, Mansa Sulayman was never able to recapture his previous good relations with Morocco. And from there on out, any real ties between the two increasingly became none existent. Rather than having a powerful friend, Mansa Sulayman would come to fear a resurgent and powerful Morocco to the north. As Mansa Musa himself had often feared, the growing threat of Morocco would become an increasing problem for the Mali Empire in the future.

Mansa Sulayman's kingdom, in the meantime, was already becoming fragmented, if not geographically, at least politically. Not everyone agreed with Sulayman replacing Mansa Musa's son Maghan, and as such, from the very beginning of his reign, not everyone supported the new emperor. When the famed Arab scholar Ibn Battuta paid a visit, he too must have soaked up much of the Malian public's disdain for the current mansa. It seems that when he first reached out to the mansa's court, he, too, became disenchanted with the monarch.

It appears that the start of Ibn Battuta's disenchantment with Mansa Sulayman occurred shortly after he contacted the emperor's royal representatives. Under normal protocol, a visiting dignitary such as Ibn Battuta would have been accorded a special welcome, which would include generous presents. Ibn Battuta no doubt knew all about the previous Mali emperor's great generosity, and he likely expected to receive something similar in kind. He was shocked when, instead of being given gifts of gold, he was just given a few loaves of bread, some beef, and a gourd filled with a hearty helping of yogurt.

He was at home when one of his fellow scholars informed him that representatives from the mansa's court had delivered a few gifts. As Ibn Battuta described it, "I got up, thinking that it would be robes of honor and money, but behold! It was three loaves of bread and a piece of beef fried in gharti [shea butter] and a gourd containing yoghurt. When I saw it, I laughed, and was long astonished at their [the Malians] feeble intellect and their respect for mean things."

It sounds pretty comical, but Ibn Battuta was downright insulted. So much so, in fact, that he dared to complain to Mansa Sulayman himself. Just imagine Ibn Battuta complaining to the great Malian leader, shouting, "Are you kidding me? I came here all the way across the Sahara, and all you have for me is a pound of beef and a couple of loaves of moldy bread?" Of course, that dialogue was a bit of an artistic flourish on this writer's part, but one can only imagine how palpable the indignation of this Arab scholar must have been.

In reality, he did not lodge his grievance directly and instead relayed his message through an envoy, and Ibn Battuta's complaint was a little more diplomatic (although still entirely indignant) than it might have been depicted above. Ibn Battuta, who followed the advice of the mansa's own griot, a court figure called "Dugha," whom Ibn referenced in his previous observations of the memorial service for the dead Moroccan sultan, gave the emperor a piece of his mind. In an official complaint sent to Mansa Sulayman, Ibn charged, "I have journeyed to the countries of the world and met their kings. I have been four months in your country without your giving me a reception gift or anything else. What shall I say of you in the presence of other sultans?"

It must have been somewhat shocking for Ibn Battuta to lodge such a complaint in regard to the mansa's hospitality. It is also a little troubling that Ibn Battuta seems to belittle him as a mere sultan when Malian mansas sought to be recognized as something more than that—they wanted to be known as powerful emperors. Mansa Musa, after all, considered himself to be at a higher level even than the sultan of Cairo. There was a reason why Musa famously refused to bow and kiss the sultan's hand, as other more subservient kings would have done. Having said that, in some ways, Ibn Battuta's words seem to have at least some measure of blatant disrespect.

Such a disrespectful discourse to an all-powerful emperor might seem pretty bold, but Ibn Battuta, who fearlessly traveled the world, was a bold person. And at least, in this case, his temerity paid off, as it has been said that by the time that he finally decided to depart company with the mansa in February of 1353, he was able to leave with his saddlebags full of "one hundred mithqals of gold."

It's important to note that the monetary unit known as the "mithqal" was actually a derivative of the Syrian currency known as the "dinar," which originated in the form of golden coins. It is said that when similar gold coins came into use in West Africa, they became known as "mithqals." Some say that the mithqal typically weighed around 4.25 grams. But this was not always the case, and there was always some variation in what a mithqal may have actually represented. Regardless, Ibn Battuta walked away with a good amount of gold.

Despite Sulayman's later gesture of goodwill, Ibn Battuta never forgot the slight and later wrote about Sulayman, saying that he was "a miserly king from whom no great donation is to be expected." But to be fair, Mansa Sulayman may have just been trying to be practical. Times were a bit different in his day than they were during the reign of Mansa Musa. Mansa Sulayman had inherited an empire much larger than the one that Mansa Musa had to contend with when he first came to the throne. Mansa Sulayman's "miserliness" was perhaps due to his concern of maintaining the cost to govern the huge frontiers of his empire.

According to West African scholar and historian William B. Noseworthy, this was a constant dilemma that Mansa Musa's successors faced. As Noseworthy puts it, "The later mansas of his [Mansa Musa] lineage struggled variously with control over the imperial economy: if they tightened spending, they would appear miserly; if they overspent, they would not retain enough funds to expand the empire." It was a sort of darned if you do and darned if you don't mentality that a lot of mansas faced when it came to the handling of their finances.

Mansa Sulayman was obviously worried about spending, and his perceived miserliness was most likely merely a kind of pragmatic caution on his part. In many ways, after all, it is much easier to build an empire than to maintain it. From the Romans to the Byzantines, from Genghis Khan to Tamerlane, all of the great sprawling empires of the world seem to be at their greatest when its rulers are still growing and annexing new territory. It is holding onto the annexed territory that becomes the hard part.

Despite his unpopularity, during his reign, Mansa Sulayman seemed well positioned for this task of consolidation. It is said that his reign was generally a peaceful and prosperous one. He still had much wealth as it pertained to gold, copper, and salt mines. From the northern Malian city of Teghaza alone, Mansa Sulayman regularly pulled in tremendous profits from the salt that was being mined. Ibn Battuta, who visited the town during his stay in the Mali Empire, famously complained, "This is a village with nothing good about it. It is the most fly-ridden of places!"

But fly traps like these brought in steady revenue for the kingdom all the same. So, it most certainly wasn't that Mansa Sulayman was broke when it came to his reasoning behind his perceived stinginess; it seems he was just trying to conserve as many resources as he could. And, as was demonstrated by Ibn Battuta's colorful testimony, with a little effort, Mansa Sulayman could still be goaded into acts of huge generosity all the same.

Before he left, Ibn Battuta also got his fair share of scandal and intrigue from the royal court. During his famous visit to the mansa's court, Ibn Battuta witnessed a falling out between Mansa Sulayman and his wife, Qasa (also spelled as Kassi). Although the mansa of the Mali Empire commonly had more than one wife, Qasa was considered to be the main royal bride of Mansa Sulayman. She was actually the niece of one of Sulayman's uncles, which made her of the royal line.

Somehow, she had fallen out of the king's favor, and Mansa Sulayman actually had her arrested and thrown in what constituted as the jailhouse. She was soon released, however, and relegated to a kind of house (or in this case palace) arrest, during which time she was closely monitored and even forced to cover her face with a veil. In the meantime, the mansa had taken a new wife by the name of Banju, who had no royal relations. Mansa Sulayman was apparently infatuated with his young new wife Banju, despite the fact that the Malian court was against it.

In fact, the mansa's advisors even went so far as to have a quiet talk with Mansa Sulayman, hoping that he would reconsider Qasa's punishment, but Mansa Sulayman refused, insisting that she had been found guilty of a grave offense. Mansa Sulayman claimed that a personal servant of Qasa was interrogated about suspicions of Qasa plotting against the king. The servant, who was bound hand and foot and subjected to questioning, allegedly confessed that Qasa was actively plotting with the king's cousin to see if he might help her depose Mansa Sulayman, pledging that the army would aid them in the cause.

It is said that once Mansa Sulayman explained these happenings to his court, they heartily agreed that the queen got what she deserved. Not only that, they insisted that if it was true, she must be put to the sword immediately. Mansa Sulayman was not willing to go that far and instead insisted on banishing her from royal affairs. Qasa would go on to live in a local mosque, where she apparently lived out the rest of her life in quiet penance and reflection.

Rather than seeming like a tyrant, Mansa Sulayman actually seemed merciful. But the question remains: was Qasa really plotting against her husband? Did her servant really testify to this? And if so, was it a false confession brought on by the duress of the interrogation?

Sadly, as with most other aspects of African history, it seems that we will probably never really know for sure.

But whatever the case may be, Sulayman's carefully orchestrated reactions during the ensuing fallout and chaos enabled him to calm his rattled court officials, prevent a possible rebellion, and save a whole lot of face in the process. From here on out, Mansa Sulayman managed to regain some of the stability that his sibling Mansa Musa had enjoyed, and he would continue to rule as the emperor for another twenty-four years.

After his death, which occurred sometime around 1360, the Mali Empire was engaged in a war of succession. This arose over disputes to the throne, with Sulayman's heir, Kanba (who also happens to sometimes be called Qasa or Kassa), and Mansa Maghan's son, Mari Diata II (also spelled as Mari Djata), each claiming the right to sit upon it. Although the details are a bit murky, it seems that Mansa Kanba may have been the relative with whom Queen Qasa had been plotting to overthrow Mansa Sulayman. At any rate, Mansa Kanba was killed after ruling Mali for less than nine months. After Mansa Kanba died, Mari Diata II ultimately came to power.

Mari Diata II would have some staying power during his time as mansa, as he remained on the throne for fourteen years. But during this time, he was widely remembered as a tyrannical leader who terribly oppressed his own subjects. He was also known as a rather frivolous, if not downright incompetent, despot who wasted precious resources.

On one occasion, for example, he supposedly sold a giant rock of pure gold, which was of immense worth, to a group of Egyptian merchants for a small fraction of its price. This feat of such squander most certainly would have had the penny-pinching Mansa Sulayman rolling over in his grave.

According to an Arab scholar named Ibn Khaldun (not to be confused with Ibn Battuta), who spoke with some of the king's subjects on the matter, most were completely aghast at what Mari Diata II was doing. Ibn Khaldun interviewed one man who is reported to have related that Mari Diata II "ruined their empire, squandered their treasure, and all but demolished the edifice of their rule."

Mansa Musa, of course, was known for his goodwill in giving away gold or even buying some provisions at marked-up rates, but Mari Diata II's hawking of this solid gold rock was apparently just considered completely pointless. Mansa Mari Diata II's rule would come to an end when he perished in his sleep in 1374. His son, who happened to be named Musa, came to power next.

But by the time of Mansa Musa II, the Mali Empire was nothing like it had been under Mansa Musa I. According to Mali historian David Conrad, Mansa Musa II was actually known to be a "just, wise, and considerate ruler," which was in stark contrast to his tyrannical predecessor, Mari Diata II. But unfortunately, Musa II just didn't seem to have the strength (or stomach) to hold the Mali Empire together.

Sometime in the middle of his reign, he opted to delegate most of his duties to a court official named Mari Jata (not to be confused with Mari Diata II). Under these conditions, Mansa Musa II was still the head of state, but his actual power was very limited. Nevertheless, his fill-in, Mari Jata, did his best to stabilize the kingdom. Among other things, he stationed troops in the Sahara Desert to keep important copper and salt mines around the city of Takedda from slipping out of the Mali Empire's grasp. For a time, he also restored authority over the eastern reaches of the empire that had since begun to break away. However, it was often an uphill struggle just to keep order in these far-flung frontiers.

In the midst of this backdrop of uncertainty, Mansa Musa II died in 1387. Mansa Musa II's brother, Mansa Maghan II, would then attempt to maintain order after Mansa Musa II's demise. He would prove even more uncomfortable with leadership, and for the short year that he reigned, he largely left major decisions up to his court ministers.

Mansa Maghan apparently died sometime in 1388, although no one seems quite sure what may have happened to him. Considering the tumultuous state of affairs in the royal capital, he very well could have been assassinated, perhaps poisoned by some court schemer. He may have also died from the so-called "sleeping sickness" that was known to befall people of all walks of life at any time during those days.

What Malians called "sleeping sickness" was actually a lethal illness that was spread by tsetse flies. These pests, which are about the size of a horsefly, actually gain their nourishment from blood, and they frequently make a snack out of grazing cattle, as well as human beings. Through this blood sucking, a dangerous parasite that lives in the fly's stomach can be transmitted, which can lead to an illness called trypanosomiasis. The illness progressively affects the victim's nervous system, and it is not uncommon for one who is affected to suddenly stop breathing in their sleep. It is for this reason that those who perish from the disease are said to have died from "sleeping sickness." Having said that, it could very well be possible that Mansa Maghan simply died in his sleep, the victim of nothing more than an errant fly that had buzzed unseen into his quarters. It has been said that countless people in the region today still fall prey to this ever-present hazard.

At any rate, after Mansa Maghan's passing, he was replaced by an ambitious court official named Sandaki. Although he was not of royal blood, he actually attempted to put some legitimacy on his reign by marrying Mansa Musa II's mother. It doesn't seem that these efforts did him much good, however, as he was assassinated a short time later. After the death of Sandaki, the empire was once again in chaos, with several factions fighting for the throne.

Amidst this turmoil, a man named Mahmud clawed his way to power in the year 1390. Unlike the usurping Sandaki, Mansa Mahmud (also known as Mansa Maghan III) had some royal blood in his veins. In fact, he could claim direct heredity from the first great Mali ruler—Sundiata Kieta. Having said that, not a whole lot is known about Mansa Mahmud's rule.

It seems that around this point, Mali became a much more isolated place, and as a result, outside commentary on the empire would become almost nonexistent. Mansa Mahmud would be the very last emperor of Mali to be specifically mentioned by name by Arab historians. After this last known mansa, who sprung from the Sundiata family tree, all available resources on Mali's subsequent imperial line seem to go completely dark. The truth is, during this period, there is a whole lot that we just don't know.

The situation only seems to deteriorate at this point, and it is recorded that the great city of Timbuktu slipped from Mali's grip in 1433. Although not many records of what happened exist, it seems that the city of Gao had already broken away a short time prior to Timbuktu leaving Mali's orbit. If Mansa Musa had lived to see all of this, he most certainly would have been heartbroken, especially considering all of the efforts he had spent in constructing majestic mosques and dynamic centers of learning in these frontiers of the former Mali Empire.

The next major phase of the Mali Empire's collapse occurred in 1460 when one of the so-called "kings" of Gao—a man who went by the name of Sulayman Dama—launched an assault on the city of Mema. After the fall of Timbuktu and Gao, Mema had become the Mali Empire's easternmost province and a storied one at that. For it was here, in the city of Mema, after all, that the great Mansa Sundiata Kiata and his noble mother, Sogolon Conde, had fled to seek refuge during a time of dynastic turmoil.

Needless to say, it came as a shock when Mema was ripped out of the Malian orbit. Mema was one of the first major provinces to become joined to the early Mali Empire, and now even Mema was lost. The Gao leader Sulayman Dama, who successfully wrested all of these lands from Mali, then proceeded to pass all of his territorial gains on to his successor, Sii Ali Beeri.

Sii Ali Beeri would carve out his own empire from the carcass of Mali and develop the next major power player in West Africa—a completely resurgent Songhai Empire. Sii Ali Beeri is said to have been an ingenious military commander, and his many successes in battle were partly due to his use of a fearsome cavalry that utilized well-armed soldiers on horseback who could quickly smash into enemy flanks. These horses were bred with the famed Barbary breed, which Bedouin raiders used on their lightning raids. Along with the rapid deployment of his horses, Sii Ali Beeri also made use of the local waterways to transport his infantry on riverboats upstream and downstream for quick mobilization.

Although Sii Ali Beeri may be considered a villain to modern-day Malians, for the Songhai, he is still considered to be a heroic figure. He is reverently known as "za beri wandu," which translates as "the great and dangerous Za." Although he was ostensibly a Muslim, Songhai storytellers contend that he was also a powerful sorcerer, hence all that talk about him being "the great and dangerous Za."

At any rate, Sii Ali Beeri was quite successful when it came to the consolidation of the gains of Gao and Timbuktu, and he forcefully reinstituted Songhai control over many of the regions' gold and salt mines. Sii Ali Beeri would go on to rule his reconstituted realm until he perished in 1492. Yes, the very year that Christopher Columbus was sailing across the Atlantic on a mission that would end up with the European discovery of the Americas, the former Mali Empire was being cast to the side by their old rival, the Songhai.

The resuscitated Songhai Empire would prove to be short-lived, however, since they were later wiped off the map by Morocco in 1591, which had invaded from the north. The fabled city of Timbuktu—Mansa Musa's pride and joy—then came under the administration of Morocco. Thus, previous Malian emperors such as Mansa Musa and Mansa Sulayman proved to be quite correct in their fear of attack from Morocco. The attack the Moroccan army launched against the Songhai in the spring of 1591 was said to have been particularly devastating. At this point, the Moroccans were well armed with muskets imported from Spain, as well as an early handgun called an arquebus. They also had some cannons that were capable of lobbing stone cannonballs.

For their part, the Songhai, who still relied largely upon the classic bow and arrow, spears, and swords, were simply no match for the upgraded weaponry of the Moroccan armed forces. The ruler of the Songhai during this time, Askia Ishaq, apparently saw the writing on the wall and attempted to literally buy himself some time. He sent a dispatch to the sultan of Morocco and pledged to pay him 100,000 pieces of gold and gift him 1,000 slaves if he would call off the assault. All this did was serve to reinforce just how demoralized and utterly defeated the Songhai were in the sultan's mind. Refusing to recall his troops, the sultan seized upon the military weakness of the Songhai and ordered his troops to seize the Songhai kingdom for Morocco.

As it pertains to the Malian dominion, the small little remnant that ultimately succeeded the Mali Empire would eventually be colonized, not by Moroccans but by Europeans. The French made inroads into what remained of Mali in 1892 during the European barnstorming epoch across the African continent known as the "Scramble for Africa." Prior to this, Mali had managed to limp on as a weak but independent state. Part of the reason behind Mali's continued resistance to colonization was its remote location, which was hard for explorers to reach.

By the late 19th century, however, the French, who already had holdings in the region, readily incorporated Mali with the rest of their colonial territories and christened the entire region as French Sudan. The French colony would then become simply known as French West Africa once more territories were cobbled together.

It is no coincidence that so many people in West Africa speak French today, as the language was imposed in many regions during France's colonization. It is somewhat ironic that much of French West Africa contained the former regions of the Mali Empire, forcing all of the puzzle pieces together that Mansa Musa and so many others had tried so hard to make fit under their own dominion. Mali would remain in this forced union of fellow colonized states until the modern-day independent nation of Mali was born in 1961.

Conclusion: The Legacy of an Empire

Throughout the history of the world, many empires have risen, and many have fallen. It is hard to say what the legacy of an empire should be. But as it pertains to the rulers of these imperial juggernauts, one man seems to stand out among them all—Mansa Musa, the tenth mansa of the Mali Empire. Even though many of the details about his life are rather scant when compared to other great leaders, what we do know is incredibly intriguing.

Mansa Musa came to power after his predecessor, Abu Bakr II, sailed across the Atlantic Ocean, never to be seen or heard from again. Like all things to do with the Mali Empire, the story of how Mansa came to the throne is epic in itself. No one knows what happened to Abu Bakr II, whether he succeeded in reaching "the other side" of the Atlantic or not, but it was on the heels of his incredible voyage that Mansa Musa came to prominence.

All evidence indicates that Mansa Musa was an ambitious king from the very beginning of his reign. He had a great interest in increasing Mali's military might and international trade, as well as in pushing the borders of the Mali Empire to farther frontiers. He also wished to be a wise and just domestic administrator, one who solved disputes and maintained a relative state of peace and order in his kingdom.

Another aspect of Mansa Musa's initiative was his earnest desire to strengthen Mali's ties to the greater Islamic world. As much as his incredible journey across thousands of miles of desert to make a pilgrimage to Mecca was meant to fulfill his personal desire to complete the hajj, he also desired to use his trip to the heart of Islam as a means to forge a lasting bond with traditional Islam.

Mansa Musa's mind was always in consideration of the betterment of his kingdom. But what is often missed about Mansa Musa's life is just how lonely his perch from the pinnacle of the Mali Empire must have been. In the Malian court tradition of the day, the emperor was considered to be so far above everyone else that it made the notion of having close, personal friendships extraordinarily difficult.

As custom dictated, the emperor was not even supposed to talk directly to his associates. All speech was to be transmitted through his court translator. While such dialogue might be almost humorous on some occasions (just imagine how difficult it would be for a mansa to request someone at a royal banquet to pass the salt), when it came to regular routine conversation with an associate, it must have been incredibly cumbersome.

But such measures were not put in place merely to make life more difficult; rather, they were in place out of sheer pragmatism. Part of the reason behind this artificial barrier between the emperor and his subjects, you see, was to make sure that no one near the ruler would unduly influence him or retain any kind of special favor. If every person who spoke to the mansa had to do so through a cumbersome, mechanical process such as this, it created the appearance of formality—nothing more and nothing less but a formal audience with the emperor.

Such formality served to keep the court gossips from assuming that anyone was being treated better than anyone else. That is not to say that these formalities ever broke down. For instance, Mansa Musa highly favored the so-called "woman from Baghdad," and it was clear to all that she was indeed someone who was very special to the emperor. Nevertheless, for the most part, Mansa Musa's daily interactions were usually highly scripted and orchestrated to keep the many tongues of his court ministers from wagging.

Following such a scripted routine must have been an incredibly daunting task, but Mansa Musa fulfilled his role. And he fulfilled it well. He was an incredibly rich and powerful man who held many secrets, and most of these alternate blessings and burdens he shouldered alone. Much of Mansa Musa's greatness lies in the fact that he was able to effectively compartmentalize his own life.

His successors were not quite so easily skilled in this department, and they were often swayed by court intrigue and led astray. His own son and then a whole litany of Mali rulers were toppled by simple excess and homegrown intrigue. And despite all of its immeasurable wealth, in the end, all the money in the world was not enough to keep the Mali Empire from falling apart. Nevertheless, the legacy of Mansa Musa and his empire continues to be imprinted and ingrained upon the Mali people to this very day.

Shortly after Mali gained independence from the French in 1961, they elected their first president: Modibo Keita. Keita was said to have been a direct descendant of that first great Keita who founded the Mali Empire, the powerful mansa Sundiata Keita. Soon after taking office, President Keita commemorated Mali's former greatness by issuing postage stamps that featured the great Sankore Mosque, one of the greatest remaining testaments to the legacy of both Mansa Musa and the Mali Empire itself.

Out of all the conglomerations of states in West Africa, the legacy of Mali is the greatest. It was only the European colony of French West Africa that came close to matching the territorial scope of the Mali Empire. And for obvious reasons, this forced entity can hardly be considered a cohesive polity by any means. What Mansa Musa and his forefathers, such as Sundiata Keita, accomplished was an incredibly unique feat in world history, and the legacy of the Mali Empire won't soon be forgotten.

Here's another book by Captivating History that you might like

Free Bonus from Captivating History (Available for a Limited time)

Hi History Lovers!

Now you have a chance to join our exclusive history list so you can get your first history ebook for free as well as discounts and a potential to get more history books for free! Simply visit the link below to join.

Captivatinghistory.com/ebook

Also, make sure to follow us on Facebook, Twitter and Youtube by searching for Captivating History.

Appendix A: Further Reading and Reference

Mansa Musa: The Most Famous African Traveler to Mecca. Barbara Krasner. 2016.

Mansa Musa I: Kankan Moussa from Niani to Mecca. Jean-Louis Roy. 2019.

Mansa Musa and Timbuktu. Charles River Editors. 2019.

Mansa Musa: Leader of Mali. Lisa Zamosky. 2007.

When Sundiata Keita Built the Mali Empire. Baby Professor. 2017.

Empires of Medieval West Africa. David C. Conrad. 2009.

The Adventures of Ibn Battuta: A Muslim Traveler of the 14th Century. Ross E. Dunn. 2012.

Mansa Musa and the Empire of Mali: A True Story of Gold and Greatness from Africa. James P. Oliver. 2013.

Encyclopedia of African History: Volume 1 A-G. Kevin Shillington. 2005.

The Quran. (Translated by M. H. Shakir). 1993.

Printed in Great Britain
by Amazon